Advance Praise for
Graced by Waters

T0060512

"John Dietsch brings us this unique collection of stories overflowing with wisdom about grief, healing, and recovery all entwined with his intimate relationship with the river."

—Robert F. ("Bobby") Kennedy, Jr.

"Dietsch manages to spring free the dusty wonder of our lives on the edge of such mystical waters and holy places—for one more precious glimpse at an evening rise—before the noche obscura of our forgetting shuts that door forever.

—Paul VanDevelder, author of *Coyote Warrior*, nominated for a Pulitzer Prize and American Book Award

"A stunningly honest and soulful work, *Graced by Waters* cuts to the conscience of angling. Many of us turn to the river for solitude, yet at the same time, concede that we never really feel alone on the water. John's writing helps to understand why that is."

—Kirk Deeter, editor-in-chief *Trout Media*/editor-at-large, *Field & Stream*

"Dietsch's book, *Graced by Waters*, showcases Mother Nature's wonderful ability to heal her broken children making them whole again. I know well…. I am one of them!"

—Andy Mill, olympian, five-time Gold Cup Tarpon Champion, and author of *A Passion for Tarpon*

"John Dietsch has created a tribute to moving water that flows like Chopin's nocturnes: timeless, transcendent, curative, universal. By turns humorous and harrowing, this luminous work is a compelling meditation on what draws us to the pulse of clear, trout-brimmed streams, and what we might learn between the banks with our own bent and dappled reflections."

—RICHARD BANGS, author of *The Lost River* and *Rivergods*

"*Graced by Waters* is a powerful reverie on Nature as both a teacher and a guide, an inseparable aspect of our humanity, and, if we allow it to be, our salvation. Dietsch's prose flows with the same clarity and grace as the rivers he describes, inviting us to reflect on our timeless and transcendent connection with water and to absorb the wisdom it provides."

—CHRIS KRESSER, M.S., *New York Times* bestselling author of *The Paleo Cure*

"As Norman Maclean wrote in his novella *A River Runs Through It*, 'Eventually all things merge into one and a river runs through it.' John, who supervised those memorable scenes in the film version of the story, reminds us that all currents converge only if and when we are willing to become open to the possibility that there is something greater than ourselves at work below the surface...I still laugh and cry out loud when I read these stories! Bravo!"

—NICOLE DARLAND, founding principal, Master Nymph/ NymphMaster and host of *Fly Fisherman TV*

"John Dietsch brilliantly brings to his readers the magic and healing power of nature: the process of fly fishing as a transformational healing force that is often dismissed as a 'hobby'....The power of water in eastern philosophy is healing and the West has lost this perspective. John reminds all of us that healing is always within our reach if we stop long enough to enjoy our river of life."

—DR. STEPHAN B. POULTER, Ph.D, clinical psychologist and author of seven books, *The Shame Factor—Heal Your Deepest Fears and Set Yourself Free*

Graced by Waters

*Personal Essays on Fly Fishing and
the Transformative Power of Nature*

JOHN DIETSCH

*Department Head for Fly Fishing
on the timeless film A River Runs Through It*

SR

A SAVIO REPUBLIC BOOK
An Imprint of Post Hill Press
ISBN: 978-1-64293-447-2
ISBN (eBook): 978-1-64293-448-9

Graced by Waters:
Personal Essays on Fly Fishing and the Transformative Power of Nature
© 2020 by John Dietsch
All Rights Reserved

Author Photo by Jennifer Cawley
Interior design and layout by Sarah Heneghan, sarah-heneghan.com

This is a work of nonfiction. All people, locations, events, and situations
are portrayed to the best of the author's memory.

posthillpress.com
New York • Nashville
Published in the United States of America

FOR MY PARENTS
Thank you for sharing your love of storytelling and nature—
and demonstrating that love, itself, is eternal.

IN THE MEMORY OF BROTHERS
Alfred Kresser Dietsch
August 5th, 1956—February 1st, 1993

Paul Stuart Dietsch
June 16th, 1963—July 27th, 1972

I will always love you.

"Something within fishermen tries to make fishing into a world perfect and apart."

—Norman Maclean
A River Runs Through It

Grief never ends
But it changes
It's a passage
Not a place to stay
Grief is not a sign of weakness
Nor a lack of faith
It's the price of love

—Unknown

"Nature is often overlooked as a healing balm for the emotional hardships (of childhood)."

—Richard Louv
Last Child in the Woods

Table of Contents

FOREWORD

Holy Waters

by Paul VanDevelder,
Pulitzer Prize-nominated author

THERE WAS A TIME NOT SO LONG AGO WHEN THE NORTHERN ROCKIES, IN general, and Missoula, Montana, in particular, marked the center of the universe for me and a lucky tribe of miscreants, vagabonds, and aimless sojourners in search of a new place to call home in the great American outback. We arrived at our various destinations in all manner of dilapidated conveyances that bristled with skis, shotguns, fly rods, pets, and bright shiny dreams recently minted by our formal induction into adulthood. From Colorado to the Canadian border, the myriad watersheds that flowed to the Gulf of Mexico and the Pacific Ocean seemed a good place to land, as good as any we'd seen; the home of cheap food, beautiful girls who could gut an elk, easy bail money, and mountain streams boiling with trout. You could make a life for yourself here, and from a high place on a clear day, you could even make out the contours of your next one.

Of course, that was back before it was discovered by Hollywood, Madison Avenue, and the wannabe lit set, but that's another story. One evening, when all things Montana were still wild and woolly, the great mystery novelist Jim Crumley asked me, "Why do you think we always come back to this place?"

I'd asked myself that question plenty of times. Jim wasn't fishing for an answer as much as he was articulating a paradox, so I floated one past him for the heck of it: "Because it's what we have instead of happy childhoods. We're all children, and children need safe places to go where they can fish and raise hell and hide out from the world when they're not busy changing it."

He flashed that inimitable Crumley grin. "That's a keeper."

My personal Montana story begins on a pastoral spring afternoon in St. Louis, Missouri. I was walking across campus to class when my favorite English professor flagged me down with a breathless request.

"My mother-in-law just broke her ankle, I've gotta deal with it, can you pick up a poet at the airport this afternoon and be his host over the weekend?"

Life can throw you breaking sliders that change the arc of personal history in an unbidden flash of grace. James Welch, a Blackfeet Indian, was in his late twenties. He had an endearing warm reserve and a velvety soft voice. Instant friendship. We drank whiskey straight out of the bottle on the banks of the Missouri River and watched the moon rise over the barge traffic. When he loosened up he told me about Montana and shared a few jagged pieces of his life story from the desolate "high line" reservation where he spent much of his childhood, the very material that would make him a singular Native American voice in American literature. And famous.

"You should come out and see Missoula for yourself," he urged me. "You'll like it. Good things are happening there."

James had just published *Riding the Earthboy 40*, his collection of poems that permanently expanded the boundaries of the known world of American poetry, and when he read them aloud in the twilight that following Monday, I'd never heard the English language do those things. I mailed my transfer application to the University of Montana, in Missoula, the following week.

In addition to sitting at the confluence of great trout rivers, Missoula had grown from a rendezvous site during the heyday of the nineteenth-century fur trade into a quaint little drinking town with two railroads and a fishing problem in the twentieth. It was the natural home of the grifter, the outsider, the flim-flam artist and con man, nomadic pool sharks, gamblers on the lam from bail bondsmen and process servers, ski bums, trust fund outlaws, and not a few professional students. Perfect home ground for a bunch of misfit writers looking for cheap digs on society's colorful fringe. Points of origin, as if any of that mattered, were planets with other names, and somehow, one by one, our various paths landed us in a town on the edge of nowhere. Paradise found. It was the first place I ever called "home."

For a time there, we were the loose sand that didn't stick to the glue when you made a sand map of the nation and shook it sideways. All of that semi-civilized detritus landed in Missoula, in particular, and the Northern Rockies, in general. That was us, the youthful *intelligencia* in exile from Berkeley, California to Madison, Wisconsin, and all parts in between, storming the ramparts of the Rockies. The *apparatchik* of local governance might well have hung an asterisk beneath the "Welcome To Missoula" sign on the road into town at Harold's Club, reading: "Normal codes of decorum and behavior governing human activity are neither observed nor enforced inside city limits."

Looking back from the vantage point of a new millennium, those years seem far too bawdy and imaginative (and faintly surreal) to describe in detail without taxing credulity. Ken Kesey, Hunter S. Thompson, Tom McGuane, Jim Harrison, Bud Guthrie, Wendell Berry, Anthony Burgess, and Truman Capote were among the wordsmiths who regularly cycled through town to drink, fish, and partake of the hilarity, while locals like Norman Maclean, Jim Crumley, Max Crawford, K. Ross Toole, Richard Hugo, William Kittredge, Jim Welch, Bill Vaughn, Peter Stark, Bryan Di Salvatore, Dorothy Johnson, Rick DeMarinis, and Steven Krauzer were imbuing the entire region with a reputation for wild-ass literary respectability. That wild-ass respectability usually involved some combination of golf clubs, fishing rods, canoes, side-by-side shotguns, rafts, hunting dogs, big coolers, borrowed cars, siphon hoses, rubber checks, and police, and there was never any way of knowing where we would end up, break down, or run out of luck, booze, money, food, or jokes, out in the high, wide, and lonesome.

What made the carnival work was good-natured grown-up townies and law enforcement officials who possessed a high tolerance for delinquent behavior and good-natured zaniness. It didn't take much to survive in style. A Pell Grant and food stamps comprised first-class tickets to the finest fishing water in the "lower 48." We were nothing if not resourceful, and now that the statute of limitations has lapsed, what seems faintly amazing is how utterly banal it all was, working as smoothly as a Swiss watch until that inevitable day that it didn't.

The credits were still running on *A River Runs Through It* when the gentile set arrived with their Orvis fishing rods and Lexuses and started building ten-thousand-square-foot starter castles on blue-ribbon trout streams. That heralded a new day, for sure, and those of us with Zebco reels and Volkswagens didn't quite know what to make of it. Somebody at the Chamber of Commerce decided the town's image needed a facelift and an attitude adjustment. Fast. Enter: fern bars and wine boutiques. Gentrification hit us like a white-out blizzard at a July picnic.

But truth be told, we knew it was coming. We knew all along. "You know, this isn't gonna last forever," I told my friend Paul one beautiful summer evening as we drove home from a day of fishing size 22 Royal Humpies on our favorite stream in the Mission Mountains. It was destined to change, but then again, so were we. Stretches of blue-ribbon trout streams that we fished during our halcyon years of "early retirement" would soon be lined with anglers from all over the world hoping to land some of that Montana magic. "One of these days it's gonna end," I told him. "They're gonna find us, and the party is gonna be over."

We were two six-packs deep into a day of glorious vistas, primordial silence, and suicidal cutthroats. He nodded. We drove along watching the light dance on the backside of the Rattlesnake Range.

"We've had a good run at it, though," he said after a while as he cracked another beer. "Come what may, a river's still gonna run through it."

And so it does, as this little book of stories attests. And despite the mess we make of human enterprise on all fronts, it bears remembering that the protagonist in all epic tales that are truly American is the land itself, that unmapped landscape of paradoxes where boundless optimism and limitless possibility run up against a bulwark of human appetites and stubborn desires, against betrayal, revenge, and, with a little luck, a measure of redemption. If you look closely, you'll almost always find water moving through that landscape, and a lone angler tying on a fresh fly in the magic hour light. Somehow, Dietsch manages to spring free the dusty wonder of our lives on the edge of such mystical waters and holy places—for one more precious glimpse at an evening rise—before the *noche obscura* of our forgetting shuts that door forever.

Preface

"In the beginning there was a river. The river became a road and the road branched out to the whole world. And because the road was once a river it was always hungry."

—Ben Okri

THE PATH THAT FOLLOWS A RIVER TO THE HEART TRANSFORMS MEN AND restores them. It takes vigilance to be totally alive; to step into this river is to seek a life in the present, and to seek a life in the present is to be graced by waters.

The more I fly fish, the more I discover its rich ability to boil down life's most complex problems into the simplest of truths. Like life, the river is constantly changing. As Heraclitus said around 500 BC, "No man ever steps in the same river twice, for it's not the same river and he is not the same man." Stepping into the river is indeed a unique moment each time, filled with anticipation and promise; nothing stays the same. Norman Maclean, author of the novella *A River Runs Through It*, wrote, "Under the rocks are the words, and some of them are theirs." These are the voices of our ancestors, and if we learn how to listen, they can transform our hearts.

I don't pretend to be a metaphysical guru, psychologist, or priest; I am a sober fisherman who has been wading through waters since he was small boy. Standing as much as I have, in rivers and other bodies of water, I have noticed that when I am very quiet, listening to the cadence of the river, watching the pull of the tide, casting to the count of the metronome in my mind or simply observing the microcosm of life that surrounds me, I become part of waters! In these moments of clarity, I am reminded that we are always, and we always have been, in exactly the right place at exactly the right time; truly, there is no other place to be than where we are at any given moment. This is the greatest lesson from waters: presence. My craft of fly fishing has taught me to observe what I see in nature and to apply it to everything in life. I believe that contained within the river and the sea is sacred energy, a power greater than ourselves. This source of life that reveals itself to us in unending lessons of discovery, healing, and renewal has often been referred to throughout time as God.*

Like many of you, I have lost loved ones. I ask the same age-old questions about all those who have come before regarding all those who will follow. Where do we go, and from where do we come? Stepping into the river I am always reminded that there is an entire world to be explored beneath the surface. Being on the water gives us unique insight into *The Great Mystery*, whether it is the tiny mayfly, who goes through several iterations in its twenty-four-hour life cycle only to lay its eggs in the same spot where it was originally born, or the massive steelhead, born from a remote freshwater stream, who swims thousands of miles back and forth across the Pacific ocean only to return and spawn in the same stretch of ancestral creek.

Interacting with these magic circles of life enriches our own and enlightens our perception. Quite simply, the art of fly fishing has helped me to pierce the veil of fear and to have faith in what I cannot see or understand; it is only without fear that we create the courage to listen, tune into our deepest intuition, become inspired, and ultimately make that cast into the unknown! As one of my mentors once told me, we can only catch a fish when our line is on the water, not floating in the air.

So what was I fishing for when I wrote the stories in this book? Frankly, when I began this process, over seven years ago, I could not see the wound that lay beneath the surface. I barely felt it tapping on my line as I plumbed the dark water; what I considered to be a grotesque creature lay hidden in the depths waiting to be transformed into something beautiful.

Like fishing, my writing required me to have courage and faith: to sit for thousands of hours discovering, discerning, and discarding. However, it was not until I wrote the final story in this anthology that I recognized the deep trauma that had been at the core of my yearning to understand: *Why do I need to fish like I do?*

As Maclean says, "How can a question be answered that asks a lifetime of questions?" My question, too, was like the one Norman asked in relation to his brother Paul's untimely death: *Do you think I could have helped him?*

For me, writing these stories down was like peeling layers from an onion, each story drilling deeper and deeper into the core of my life story. Suddenly, I realized that I had spent years avoiding my seminal story of brotherhood: about my own brother Paul's death and how I blamed myself for his passing all these years. It wasn't until seven days before the book was due to the publisher that I sat down to write the final story and recognized how all these years my soul had been displaced, even outside of my own body. All these years I had been fishing for a connection, and suddenly I found it. I knew that Maclean had waited until he was in his seventies to write about his brother Paul's death. Before that, it was too painful, he said. *I still have a couple of decades left,* I told myself. *Until then, it will be too painful.*

Perhaps I heard a whisper within the gentle coursing of the river: *Of course, you wrote these stories for a reason: You are being asked to share your grief so that others can permit themselves to explore their own.* After seven years of writing, I went back to where I first fished, and struck gold; I discovered that my *Angel with a Perfect Heart* has been with me my entire life. He is part of what I have sensed all these years when graced by waters: His were among the *words under the rocks.*

It wasn't until the end of my writing process that I recognized I was asking the wrong questions. I had become like a detective turning over thousands of rocks trying to find the right words for the answer, to no avail. So I went back to the original question I asked: *Why do I need to fish like I do?* And the answer I got back was quite revealing: it turns out that neuroscience has discovered that the best therapy for childhood trauma is *play*, and what better form of play than fishing? Play is typically engaged in more for enjoyment and recreation than practical purpose. It takes us back to our days as children when romping in streams, fields, and neighborhoods was undertaken for pure pleasure and discovery. Most adults have lost their ability to play, but now even medical science is proving the essential need for play in our lives, *especially those of us who suffered childhood trauma*. After writing this book, I have come to see that my obsessive need to play and my passion for fishing all these years may have even saved my life.

In the beginning, I learned from my mentor how to tie a fly to the line and cast it. At first, I could not see. I had to train my mind to perceive what I could not, looking for something hidden beneath the surface. At first I was illiterate. However, once I knew the basic vocabulary of the river I could begin to read it. When I knew what to look for, the signs were everywhere, and suddenly what used to look like barren water revealed itself to me. Slowly, I began to interpret its currents, and the river rewarded me for my wisdom: not just a fish to the net, but a connection to the natural and supernatural as pure and intangible as the river itself.

At first, as a beginner, I made lots of mistakes. I struggled to let go of that incessant chatter in my head insisting "you failed"; however, when I surrendered to the moment, I discovered that my struggle often had a dividend: insight. It seemed to be born from the Zen-like focus I developed from the repetitive motion of fly casting while single-mindedly concentrating on my fly as it floated down the river. Failure became essential for learning and eventually led to success: first one fish then another and another. Success required me to focus at a higher level, letting go of doubt, using stealth, and placing the fly artfully just above my intended target so it would float down naturally with the current.

I had no chance of connecting with what I could not see unless I had the courage to explore the depths, trained with diligence, and employed skillful means to approach the unknown. Perhaps the same can be said of our souls.

Grief leads to forgiveness, forgiveness leads to acceptance, and acceptance leads to faith: belief in the face of credible doubt.

Wading on this side of the river can be precarious. Because the pools and runs here on this side are deeper, they often feel more numinous. Don't be fooled by the illusion of safety projected by the shallows on the far side! Exploring the deepest pools in the river is not without risk, but this is where we fish for what was lost.

As frightening as the depths may seem, the biggest risk of all is choosing *not* to wade this side of the river, then looking back some day in regret, having wished that we had had the courage to wade and fish its most challenging pools. For most, the shallows on the opposite bank, where minions can be seen casting, provide a constant illusion that the catching must be better *elsewhere*. However, staying in the process of fishing always brings more results than daydreaming about the catch. On this side of the river, it is better to have fished and failed than to have never fished at all.

Even if we get what we *think* we came for, holding onto something we love as though it is ours to keep forever, we must let it go. In the end we must let go of everything. This is the universal law of catch and release: Nothing really belongs to us except our capacity to love.

I believe this is the message contained in the melodic whispers of each coursing eddy and rolling wave. Waters speak their own language; the more time we spend fishing, the more likely we are to find *words under the rocks*, perhaps from our loved ones, that speak to our hearts. These are the lessons I have learned from rivers. They remind us that we are them and they are us; we are all graced by waters.

*A note about the word "God": When I set out writing these stories about my connection to waters, I did not intend to use the word God. *Using*

the word God will alienate agnostics, atheists, and anglers, I thought. However, when I tried using other words like *Universal Mind, Super Intelligence, Divine Master,* or *The River,* it just didn't work! The result is that I now use the word God more than sixty times in the book (not counting other references to words like *Higher Power, Spirit,* and *Source*). While I don't want to isolate my description of God to one ineffective sentence, I think I can boil it down to this: *the universal power we feel when we recognize how we are all a part of something much greater than our ourselves.* To me this describes the very source of waters: our own collective soul. If you still have a challenge with the G-word I might suggest that you translate the term God into *Good Orderly Direction*: that invisible force that often works in our lives once we recognize that everything, in the end, works out the way it's supposed to, moment by moment, the same way that water flows, one day at a time.

CHAPTER 1

Canyon Wisdom

In the Canyon of My Brother's Keeper

"Many of us would probably be better fishermen if we did not waste so much time watching and waiting for the world to be perfect."

—Norman Maclean

I RECENTLY READ ABOUT THE BROTHER OF A MURDERED SOLDIER, ONE OF many who have been killed in Afghanistan by fellow Afghani army men who suddenly turned on their American counterparts. My first instinct was anger at the senseless murder. As I kept reading, I thought about how emotionally distraught the surviving brother must be over this terrible act of traitor-based terrorism, but when a reporter asked him how he felt about the situation, he answered, "I do not know what was in the heart of the man who killed my brother. I don't know what he was seeking. Those are things that I am going to have to leave to a Higher Power. If I dwell on it, I let it take over."

I have often had the same thoughts since losing both of my brothers. Wondering to myself why this happened to this particular brother in the newspaper article, I realized that I was asking the question to the wrong person; the only one who can answer such questions is God.

When it comes to matters of providence and loss, my anger often wants to blame God for making the world such a vicious place. Luckily, when I get out to the stream and surround myself with the beauty of nature and the sounds of the divine, my anger over what I have lost dissipates and I see what I have—and it is enough.

I miss my brothers every day, but it does not mean that I have to shut off remembering them. Perhaps, the initial anger that I had toward my Higher Power for *allowing* my brothers to die prevented me from seeing that I was powerless over their deaths. Unless I put faith in a power greater than myself regarding those answers, I was doomed to dwell on that question and let it take me over, just as the soldier's brother warned. Faith is a precious commodity and perhaps the most important element in our lives. We can lose jobs, money, wives, parents, or loved ones and we survive. We can even learn to thrive. If we lose faith, however, we have nothing.

The story of *A River Runs Through It* is like the Holy Grail for millions of anglers, and for me it is no different. Its author, Norman Maclean, took nearly his entire lifetime to find the courage to write about the traumatic experience of losing his brother. He was past the age of seventy when he finally sat down to write about his brother's passing; perhaps it took him that long to process the loss and come to grips with his powerlessness over it. Yet the question throughout his story seems to ask: *Was there something more I could have done to prevent my brother from dying?*

At one point in the story Norman writes, *"Many of us would probably be better fishermen if we did not waste so much time watching and waiting for the world to be perfect."* The river asks us to accept life on life's terms, not our own—this is our path no matter how hard it might be to accept—sometimes the giant boulders and washed-out sections seem impossible to cross. We are powerless over factors like weather, water temperature, and any number of catastrophic events that might take place. We are also powerless over what people and fish may or may not do. Life is imperfect and so are we, but the river reminds us that there is a form of perfection in the ever-changing moment that is the *process* of fishing. Progress, not perfection.

One time in New Zealand, while making a TV show, I was casting to a double-digit (that is, ten pounds or over) brown trout when the guide and I suddenly saw it sink out of sight. Within two minutes the river started rising rapidly and within a half hour it went up nearly ten feet (which was all caught on camera)! I still blame myself for not catching that fish before the flash flood hit, but the reality is that this kind of thinking is due to excessive pride as though I were God and could influence the flood or the fish.

"Yet even in the loneliness of the canyon I knew there were others like me that had brothers they did not understand but wanted to help," Maclean writes. *"We are probably those referred to as 'our brother's keepers,' possessed of one of the oldest and possibly one of the most futile and certainly one of the most haunting of instincts. It will not let us go."*

As a card-carrying member of the "Brother's Keeper" club, I want to believe that I have the power to save people I love from themselves or from certain demise. Metaphorically, when I can clearly see that they have strayed from the waters I think they *should* be fishing, I feel it is my duty to straighten them out. Only recently have I come to see that this is *not* my role. Just like a fish may not take my fly, so may a loved one refuse my help. I have to let go of the results without giving up on the process. I am a good fisherman and hopefully I can allow God to work through me, but only if "I" get out of the way and go with the flow.

Norman addresses this dilemma by using his brother's fly fishing as a metaphor. When Norman is catching fish, but his brother Paul is not, Norman writes, *"I was thinking of how, when things got tough, my brother looked to get himself out of trouble. He never looked for any flies from me.... I started by thinking, though he was my brother, he was knot headed. I pursued this line of thought back to the Greeks who believed that not wanting any help might even get you killed."*

In the end, we can offer help but there is never any assurance that someone will accept it; if our help is not sought by someone in trouble, then what? This, perhaps, is the acceptance we need to seek from our own Higher Power: to help us see that we are powerless in this regard. Unless I can detach with love, I am destined to become mired in thinking I can solve someone else's problem.

Arguably, Norman's brother Paul was eventually murdered because of his addiction to gambling. He couldn't pay his debts and his excessive pride left him unwilling to ask for help. We are led to believe that Paul was killed by an angry bookie. However, the murder was never solved. It is still possible, to this day, that Paul was killed by a random act of violence, like the murdered soldier in the news story I read.

In all cases of death, the pattern appears to be random. No matter if someone has a drinking, gambling, food, or other addiction that causes his or her demise, whether they die from cancer or a psychological disorder—or suddenly for no apparent reason—we may ask: *Was there something we could have done to prevent it from happening?* This question is amplified when addiction, disease, or an accident that *we think was preventable* is the underlying cause of the affliction.

What do we have power over? Over what or whom are we powerless? Do we have the wisdom to know the difference? Reverend Maclean, Paul's father, tries to answer this question when he asks:

"'Do you think I could have helped [Paul]?' [my father] asked. Even if I had thought longer, I would have made the same answer. 'Do you think I could have helped him?' I answered. We stood in deference to each other. How can a question be answered that asks a lifetime of questions?

"It is those we live with and love and should know who elude us," Norman's father concludes.

At the end of our long journey, when we reach the terminus of that box canyon where the waters bubble up from eternal springs beneath the tall cliff, it will come down to one thing, and that is, how we loved.

While wading the river, we pursue things of value. Along the way, we can hopefully be of service by passing our wisdom on to our fellow anglers and others we meet along the way.

By looking to the skies above, past the immensity of the cliffs surrounding us and the billowing clouds casting shadows on the runs and riffles ahead, we ask for the courage to look below: to go beneath the surface where our eyes cannot see, to give us better perspective on how to navigate the various currents of the river ahead, and perhaps for guidance on where we might cast our line. We ask that our insight from the outside be transformed into our own innate intuition on the inside.

Along the way, we honor those who have gone before us, knowing that they have now become the river itself; they are magical molecules recycling throughout the earth with a heavenly bond to the Great Creator who will also reclaim our souls when we are called.

> *"Eventually all things merge into one and a river runs through it. The river was cut by the world's great flood and runs over rocks from the basement of time. On some rocks are timeless raindrops. Under the rocks are the words, and some of the words are theirs.*
> *"I am haunted by waters."*
>
> —Norman Maclean,
> *A River Runs Through It*

The Fly Fishing Stunt Man[1]

It was late in the afternoon in Livingston. As I drove over the pass toward Bozeman, I realized there was no sense scouting locations; dark rain clouds hung over the Gallatin Mountains to the West where I was headed. I turned around and drove back to the set, where Robert Redford and the crew were shooting the scene from *A River Runs Through It* where Brad Pitt's character Paul Maclean sits on the courthouse steps and says, "The world is full of bastards, the number increasing rapidly the further one gets from Missoula, Montana."

As I approached the set it began to rain. Several grips rushed to cover the film equipment and lights.

A production assistant came up to me and said that Redford wanted to meet with me in his trailer "ASAP." The rain had shifted our schedule.

I had been waiting for this meeting for six weeks—a month and a half of scouting locations on the Blackfoot, Gallatin, and Boulder rivers, teaching the actors to cast, poring over the script, and creating storyboards to make sure the fishing scenes made sense. I placed all this information in my big red notebook...*that I left back at the office in Livingston!*

I made a panicked call to have a PA drive the notebook over the pass, which would take at least half an hour. Unprepared and nervous, I walked into the nondescript white trailer.

---

1   Excerpted *from Shadowcasting: An Introduction to the Art of Flyfishing* (2000). Reprinted with permission from Clinetop Press.

"Hey, Bob," I said. Everyone called Robert Redford "Bob."

Redford is much shorter than you might imagine, but what he lacks in height he makes up for in spades with his disarming smile, rugged good looks, and the kind of hair that a balding guy like me covets!

"Hello," Bob said, warmly welcoming me into his makeshift office.

He shifted and producer Patrick Markey, production designer Jon Hutman, and screenwriter Richard Friedenberg scooted over to make room for me at the table. The rain struck the roof with a melodious pitter-patter as Redford talked about the fishing scenes. He had a definite vision and expressed ideas with the kind of grace that made him famous.

In the film industry, Redford is known for delegating. He and Markey had asked me to mastermind the choreography of the fishing scenes, then basically cut me loose to work with the location department and my assistant Jason Borger. We drew up the storyboards based on the collective vision that Redford and Patrick had for those scenes and from feedback from members of the fly fishing team, including John Bailey from Dan Bailey's Fly Shop in Livingston, as well as Jerry Siem, who at the time was rod designer for Winston Rod Company.

Redford always had a general view of how things should look. The various department heads were expected to execute their visions and, as the head of the world's first fly fishing film department, I knew that the details of his vision would fall into place once I laid out my initial thoughts. Redford was a master filmmaker and I was about to share my ideas with him on perhaps the greatest fly fishing story ever told. It should have been one of the defining moments of my career, except for the fact that my notes were in a car traveling somewhere over Bozeman Pass.

Time passed quickly as we discussed the scenes and before I knew it, there was a knock on the door. I breathed a sigh of relief when the PA arrived with my notebook just in time.

Redford then went through the detailed storyboards of each fishing sequence Jason and I had envisioned. Knowing that we planned to shoot the scenes just above Squaw Creek Bridge in Gallatin Canyon, he took our sketches and gave us a more detailed vision for how he wanted the scenes to be shot, suggesting different angles and adding subtext. After going through each scene, he suddenly skipped to the last sequence and looked up at me.

"Is there anything different we can do with the final fishing scene?" he asked point-blank. "The way it's written in the book and the script, it's too much like the other scenes. We need something more exciting." His voice trailed off.

A long pause ensued; I knew he was looking for a solution I had yet to consider. I had to think fast. From a dramatic point of view, the problem with the last fishing scene in the book (and the first draft of the screenplay) was the way Norman's brother Paul catches the large fish while fishing from the far bank; once he lands a big rainbow, he decides to wade across the river in a swift section instead of walking down below and crossing where it is safer. On his way across, he slips and goes under for a moment. For Maclean, it was a subtle way to foreshadow his brother's impending death. But for Redford it was too subtle, with too little differentiation from the other fishing scenes.

"It needs to have more of an edge," he added.

Then it came to me.

"What if Paul sees a huge fish just below a rock at the top of a big rapid," I said with enthusiasm (retelling a fish story told to me by my buddy Thomas Lockie when he swam under a bridge on the Big Hole River to land a trout). "He tries to get a good drift, but the fish won't take. The fly is dragging because of the swift current between him and the pool where the fish is," I said, shooting from the hip. "He needs to get closer to get a better drift, so he inches out to the edge of the seam on the rapid, barely holding on. His feet are slipping. Perhaps we see that from down below with an underwater shot," I conjectured. "By getting right on the edge of the eddy line, he can now keep the rod high enough to keep the leader just above the fast water to get a decent drift. He casts. The fly lands gently…."

I paused for effect. "Perhaps he casts but can't get a good enough drift, so he has to get even closer to the fast-moving rapids, and maybe his feet start to slip as he casts again," I said, pausing again, starting to stand and using hand gestures as though I were fishing "...And kerpow! This huge 'bow erupts out of the water, takes the fly, and screams downstream in an explosive run." I stood up all the way and leaned back, holding up my arm like I was playing the fish.

"Paul tries to play the fish from where he is, but it's huge. It screams downriver, into his backing. We cut to his boots slipping in the gravel beneath the surface. The Brad character makes a split-second decision to enter the river. In order to keep the fish on, he has to *swim* the rapid while playing the fish." I stopped. After a short pause, Redford looked me right in the eye.

"And then what?" he asked. It was as if I had just hooked a big fish myself!

I wasn't sure where to take the rest of the story but felt like it was my job to complete the idea, so I hemmed and hawed and explained that Paul would swim the rapid, fight through the waves, and negotiate the rocks. At the end of the fight, he would stand up in the tail of the pool and hoist the behemoth trout in the air, grinning.

"Do you know where we'd shoot this?" Bob asked, obviously interested.

"Yeah, I think I know the exact spot," I replied.

After the meeting, at the foot of the trailer's step, Patrick chewed me out for pitching something to the director without passing it by him first.

"Do you know how much this is gonna cost?" he asked through clenched teeth.

This time I just kept quiet and shook my head, remembering one of the key adages in the film production world: *Sometimes it's better to beg for forgiveness afterward than ask for permission beforehand.*

The next day, I traveled out to the section of river I had seen weeks before: a classic piece of class-three whitewater about a half-mile above

Squaw Creek Bridge. There, accompanied by the whitewater rescue team that stood by in their kayaks, I donned a wetsuit, mustered up courage, and with a weighted plastic bottle at the end of my line swam the rapids playing an imaginary fish while Jason filmed me on a VHS camcorder. After showing Redford the footage and unsuccessfully trying to have a Hollywood stuntman swim the rapid while playing a fish in the same way, Redford asked me to do the actual stunt in the film.

The day of the shoot, shortly after filling out my Taft-Hartley paperwork to become part of the Screen Actors Guild, I walked along the banks above the rapids scouting the path I would swim through the rocks. Across the way, nearly a hundred crew members set up equipment. Dressed in the exact same period outfit as Brad Pitt, but with a thin skin-colored wetsuit underneath, the nerves in my belly jumped around like fish fry. I could see a bunch of the office staff on the other side. *They're here to watch me kill myself,* I thought. With all the money being spent (to Patrick's chagrin), I only had one shot to get it right. We had gone through this dozens of times on paper. Jerry Siem planned to drop a small weighted plastic bottle, attached to my fly line, into the rushing water thirty feet ahead of me to simulate the running fish. This would put weight on my rod to imitate the fighting fish. It had worked just right in rehearsal so, having done it once before on video, I was surprised by my lack of faith. My old friend, self-doubt, began to creep in.

A French voice spoke behind me. "So now you're a stuntman."

I turned around and realized that Philippe Rousselot, Director of Photography, had been walking behind me the whole time.

"Look, John," he said, sensing my doubt. "I have filmed stuntmen jumping off cliffs in Switzerland for *The Bear* and fighting in the jungles of South America for *The Emerald Forest,* but I have never killed anyone. I don't intend to now."

After an awkward pause, he asked, "Are you going to die?"

"What?" I laughed nervously, relieved at his sick humor. I was about to swim a class-three rapid without a helmet or life vest, but I replied with as much confidence as I could gather. "I'm sure it's safe, Philippe."

"Good. We go to have five takes," he replied in broken Franglish.

My jaw dropped as he turned around brusquely and left.

I had expected to swim the rapid once, maybe twice. Then I remembered. This was show business.

As I stared blankly at the huge crane hanging over the whitewater, I imagined the camera capturing my demise. John Bailey sensed my hesitation and walked over. "You'll be fine," he said. I waded out into the water and positioned myself on top of a large boulder at the head of the rapid. As the cameras rolled, Bailey signaled Jerry to drop the bottle. The assistant director yelled "Action!" and I jumped into the frigid water.

I was immediately swept into a channel. I aimed for the camera as best I could but the bottle was not in front of me. It was behind! The fly line tightened and spun me around. The rod shot out of my hands and a massive wave smashed me under the water, upside down.

Everything went silent. I waited for the current, perhaps listening for the words of my ancestors beneath the rocks in the river that Maclean wrote about. I relaxed and waited for the end.

Then the words came. They were my own: "Jesus Christ!" I screamed as I came to the surface, gasping for air and dog paddling to the edge of the pool. One of the river safety guys yanked me from the water and asked if I was alright.

"Yeah," I told him. "I'm fine."

I flunked my first attempt as a true fly fishing stuntman. And now the stunt rod was missing! Luckily, Bailey was able to find the weighted bottle. It had caught itself in a crack between two rocks. He was able to trace the fly line and retrieve the $1,500 custom rig intact.

We did four more takes. As it turned out, the initial mistake we made ended up being exactly what the editor needed to give the sequence more suspense. She was able to use the shot where I hit the wave and disappeared in the final cut showing Brad Pitt's character being submerged underwater. Like me, the character disappears for several seconds while everyone wonders if he will pop back up or not.

Ever since my pitch in Redford's trailer, we hadn't figured out how to end the actual swimming part of the sequence. Now, by total accident, we had an ending that would be remembered by generations of fly fishermen and movie-goers. In the actual film, it looks like Brad Pitt's character practically drowns because I practically drowned!

With the help of a second-unit team that went back to those roiling rapids in the fall of 1992 and shot inserts, then coupled those shots with existing footage of the father and Norman looking out at the rapid, the scene became infamous. While most people like the way we adapted the novella for the screen, I have had the occasional aficionado tell me that we went over the top. For me, that particular adaptation was the biggest mark I made on the film.

In a special outdoor issue of *Esquire* magazine, released just before the film opened eighteen months later, I saw three photographs that were taken of me from a distance while I did the stunt. The caption read, *"Brad Pitt swims the river while playing a fish in* A River Runs Through It.*"*

Today, nearly thirty years later, my grey hair betrays the resemblance to the young man that swam those rapids. Like Norman, I find myself reflecting about those long-ago times on the river and, like the adage on the film's poster, I know that "Nothing perfect lasts forever. Except in our memories."

> *Then in the Arctic half-light of the canyon, all existence fades to a being with my soul and memories and the sounds of the Big Blackfoot River and a four-count rhythm and the hope that a fish will rise. Eventually, all things merge into one, and a river runs through it.*
>
> —Norman Maclean,
> *A River Runs Through It*

Rod of Redemption

Jesus replied, "You do not realize now what I am doing, but later you will understand."

—John 13:7

I REMEMBER PREPARING FOR A BACKPACKING TRIP ONE DAY IN EARLY JULY many moons ago. I planned to go fishing with a friend in the Black Canyon of the Gunnison River near Montrose, Colorado. As always, the key ingredient for a trip like this was my trusted four-piece, six-weight graphite fly rod, contained in a metal tube with the words "High Performance Scott Fly Rods" from the company that has often sponsored my fishing programs across the planet. The rod's fast action and stout character made it the perfect tool for plying the fast waters and big fish in the canyon. I thought to myself, *this is my magic wand, the one I wave in a very specific manner, having been taught by so many wizards along the way, to manifest beings on the river.*

After a three-hour drive from Aspen, my good friend Paul and I parked at the top of the Long Draw Trail (also known as Devil's Slide). Getting out of Paul's circa 1970 Toyota Land Cruiser, we walked to the edge and peered into the Black Canyon.

"My God," I said, looking out over the vastness of the snake-like green and white ribbon of water carving its way beneath the dark sheer cliffs close to two thousand feet below. "I forgot how *huge* this place is."

"Let's get the backpacks and go," Paul said abruptly, seemingly un-affected by the view. Watching him walk back to the Land Cruiser, his beat-up Stetson cowboy hat bobbing with impatience, I thought back to when we met, my first year of guiding in the Fothergill's Fly Shop where he'd been hired to work booking trips and helping customers in the heart of Aspen. A Wisconsin native, Paul was a couple of years younger than me and about as down-home a guy as you could ever meet: a blue-collar, hard-working, matter-of-fact outdoorsman with a wicked sense of humor and a genuine smile. He was more of a spin-fisherman in those early days, always wanting to add drops of a fish attractor called Dr. J (short for Juice) to his flies because he was convinced that fish only ate things that smelled like bait. I felt obligated at first to help him learn more about fly fishing, but it wasn't long before Paul's Midwestern insights and hunting instincts transformed him into one of the best fly fishermen in the Valley. Mornings, while waiting for clients in the shop, if I snuck into the tiny bathroom for a spell, I could hear Paul shout out to the other guides waiting for clients, "There goes Dietsch having a Mister Coffee!" I think every fisherman worth his salt has his number one fishing buddy. For me it has always been Paul.

Standing on the rim of the canyon, I resisted the fish greed for a moment and opted instead to take it all in: the lofty clouds in the bright blue sky, the barely audible sound of the roaring river in the distance, and the sweet smell of damp sage that carried with it all the memories of fishing here in this canyon from years past. My mind wandered to huge rainbows, up to six pounds. I knew they were there in the canyon below because I'd caught them before. They hid deep in the throats of the biggest runs. I imagined them slowly rising up to my big Sofa Pillow pattern, eating what they thought was a salmon fly the size of my index finger.

"Dietsch, *let's go!*" Paul yelled as he pulled his pack from the car and me from my reverie. I quickly ran to the car, fumbled desperately with my gear, and threw my pack on my back, hoping he wouldn't get too far ahead!

Paul and I had fished many other places in the canyon but this was the first time we had tried this particular section. From talking with others who have made the descent, Slide Trail was reputed to be a son of a bitch (not to be confused with SOB, the name of a similar trail nearby). Within minutes the trail disappeared. Suddenly, we found ourselves staring down a steep forty-degree slope, only thirty feet in width, cut into the sheer rock cliff, strewn with massive boulders the size of Volkswagens. Even from this height we could see the river, some 1,800 feet below.

At first the going was very slow and treacherous. We had to be vigilant about each placement of our feet as some of the boulders were loose and required that we sit down before sliding down to the next shelf. Falling was not an option.

About halfway down, the sound of the river increased. I traversed across a narrow section of rock, my back against the wall, ten feet above the next boulder below. I momentarily forgot about my wide berth as the backpack brushed against the granite and pushed me to the precipice. I lost my balance and butterflies invaded my stomach as I struggled to keep from falling. That moment seemed to last an eternity as I contemplated the grim possibility of pain or death. But within seconds I regained my balance and moved on.

Without question, the Gunnison River is still one of the most beautiful places in the world. Arriving at the bottom of the grade was now all the more gratifying considering the labor and danger of the ninety-minute descent. Seeing the grace and roar of the river renewed our excitement, until I opened my rod tube. I reached in to pull out a modern graphite high-performance instrument. Instead, I pulled out an unfamiliar case. My heart sank immediately. What was this? It looked like my grandfather's old bamboo fly rod, and when I untied the strings of the case and unfurled the top, the butt section I pulled out was indeed not a fast-action Scott, but instead, a circa 1930 clunker! Although the rod had been restored it was heavy and slow, a far cry from the lightweight, fast-action rods that allowed me to cast with the precision I needed to target big rainbows in the canyon. I had been looking forward to fishing this canyon for months now, going through the experience in my mind over and over again, creating the kind of expectation that now fueled my resentment over the stupid mistake I had apparently made. *My trip is ruined*, I thought to myself. Looking around the canyon I suddenly felt trapped by its walls. Gripping the butt section of the old bamboo rod instead of my high-performance Scott was like finding myself gripping the steering wheel of a jalopy instead of a Formula One race car.

Somehow the old rod ended up in the wrong tube. Apparently, I never checked to see what rod was inside before I took it down from the attic. When Paul saw the look on my face, and the bamboo rod in my hand, he could not help but laugh. I had a reputation for being forgetful and he thought this was pretty funny. Apart from my embarrassment, my mind convinced me that I was now handicapped, and that Paul would catch the most and biggest rainbows. I went immediately to my competitiveness and what I lacked, forgetting momentarily that I was holding my grandfather's heirloom in my favorite spot on the planet.

Then Paul said, "Maybe it's meant to be."

He said it half in jest, and my ensuing laughter helped to get me out of my head…. I was present again, holding a fly rod in the middle of one of the most beautiful canyons in the world. I smiled and a trans-formation began. These are the cards that I had been dealt and rather than beat myself up about it, why not have some fun?

I marveled at the beauty of the rod butt, the mid-section, and tip, running my hands over the carefully crafted bamboo. The rod seat looked like it was made of nickel with a totally enclosed metal fixture at the butt that rotated to fit the reel in place. The guides were all neatly wrapped in bright red silk capped with thin black trim between the wrap and bamboo. The bamboo itself was six-sided like a pencil with three sections: eighteen pieces of perfectly tapered slices of bamboo glued, cut into three separate pieces, engineered to fit together perfectly to form this wand-like device. I swirled each of the three metal ferrules across the crease next to my nose to grease them before slipping each of the three males into their female counterparts. Once complete, I flexed the eight-foot rod back and forth to check its action: it felt *much* heavier, shorter and slower than the modern nine-foot graphite rods to which I had grown accustomed. Suddenly my curiosity turned to frustration: *I have to fish with this for two days?* The answer came back: *yes.*

Years before, I did some research about this old Wright and McGill eight-foot *Favorite* rod that belonged to my departed grandfather, and I discovered it was a mass-produced model from the 1930s and not worth very much. Nonetheless, out of respect for this heirloom, I shipped it to Len Codella, who I had hired to consult on, source, and restore, all the classic fly fishing tackle on *A River Runs Through It*. Len concurred that the rod was not valuable from a monetary standpoint but we both agreed that it was priceless as a keepsake. He offered to restore it to look like one of the rods that the Maclean brothers would have used.

Len had wrapped the Sweetheart's guides in the crimson red colors with black trim to look somewhat like Norman Maclean's rod. Back in 1992, while in pre-production, I spoke to Len about a rod that George Croonenberghs, a consultant on the film, called "The Montag." Croonenberghs, who often fished with the Macleans, told me that Norman fished exclusively with this model. We planned to have Len restore nine rods to imitate the ones that Maclean described (three sets for each character) in his famous novella, but he had never heard of a "Montag." For weeks I tried to figure out how it was that George Croonenberghs, who tied flies for the Maclean brothers and is mentioned in Norman's novella, swore that Norman fished with a rod that one of the world's most knowledgeable fly rod historians had never heard of. George told us that Paul, Norman's brother, fished with a nicer bamboo rod, and from the description, Len figured it was a Goodwin or a Wright and McGill *Granger*. On the other hand, Norman's "Montag" rod remained a mystery.

Because affordable bamboo rods from that era were clunky, we had a rod designer named Walton Powell build us an additional set of nine Hexagraph replicas made of graphite that imitated the bamboo rods but were lighter and easier to cast for the actors and doubles. George got a little irritated with me after I asked one too many times if he were "triple sure" that "Montag" was the name of the rod Norman used. He insisted that indeed it was.

Finally, I got a call from Len.

"I think I figured out what rod Norman Maclean used," he said with a laugh. "I was looking at the old Montague rods here in the shop and suddenly realized that George and the Macleans must've pronounced the Montague as 'Montag!'"

At the bottom of the canyon, with this backstory in mind and rod in hand, I imagined this instrument as a magic wand transforming what I perceived as a mistake into an honor; the last person to cast this beautiful bamboo rod was my grandfather fifty years ago. Now it was my turn.

When I looked down at the carefully wrapped guides, the metallic ferrules, and the six-sided craftsmanship, I detected something impalpable within my grasp. I wondered why I hadn't fished the rod before, then heard the words "meant to be" wafting up from the melodious sound of the river....

"Meant to be!" Paul said again, laughing as he made a thirty-foot cast with his graphite Scott and hooked a hefty brown trout. "Check it out," he remarked, pointing to a two-inch long salmon fly crawling along the base of his fly rod. "They're still in here," Paul said, referring to the fact that the trout's favorite food was still in and around the banks of the canyon. It was early July and depending on the weather, the salmon flies in this part of the river were sometimes long gone by now. A snap of cold weather earlier in the month had evidently allowed them to stay around.

My excitement reignited, I searched through my vest, found my box of large flies, opened the case, and selected a massive Sofa Pillow pattern to match the natural stonefly. "At least I brought the right flies," I mumbled as I rigged the antique rod with my fly line, lucky that the six-weight line I'd brought for my graphite rod matched the *Favorite*. When I completed the task, I eagerly tied the Sofa Pillow onto the end of my line. The rod felt heavy and awkward as I made my way down to the river. I caught myself again and shifted the thought to the magic that might be contained within an heirloom passed down from my grandfather.

Bamboo is a revered plant in many parts of Asia and in the Tonkin region, where the best "fly rod" bamboo is harvested. Over the centuries, this member of the grass family has been interwoven into the spiritual lives of the human family. Not only is bamboo often used as part of the final birthing process for many Asians, it is also present in death; bamboo caskets have carried the dead into the next world for thousands of years.

Many aboriginal cultures consider bamboo the ultimate totem for those seeking increased mental flexibility and spiritual growth. Some of the best bamboo fly rod makers, who are around this material day in and day out, believe that there is a spiritual quality captured within the final result of their craftsmanship, one that could never compare to a composite rod like graphite.

The Druids, priest-like magicians who lived in the British Isles beginning around the time of Christ, believed that their gods lived in trees and are the central reason for the phrase still used today: "Knock on Wood." (The Druids also believed that when our loved ones pass on they are still with us, every day, which is why many Irish Catholic priests believe and teach the same principle—to accept this kind of faith and believe we are never alone.) While bamboo is technically a grass and not a wood, the notion that the material itself might conduct some sort of spiritual or magical power of transformation is a myth that transcends time.

I watched for a moment as Paul disappeared around the corner downstream. I was alone now and as I looked across the roaring rapids in front of me, I felt that familiar pit in my stomach. I paused for a moment and surveyed the tail out section of the giant run where I planned to cross. The Gunnison is a powerful river. Even at four hundred cfs (cubic feet per second), crossing the Gunnison in waders can be life-threatening. This river comes out of the bottom of Blue Mesa Reservoir, some thirty miles to the south and east. It drops at an average of thirty-four feet per mile, making it the fifth steepest mountain descent in North America. Inside the canyon, that translates to lots and lots of dangerous white water.

There were few places to cross safely, but after scouting with Paul, we decided that I should cross at the tail out of the upper rapids. I half expected that Paul would wait on the near bank to be sure I got across safely, but now that he was gone, I cinched up my wading belt, and stepped into liquid.

The dead weight of the current soon pushed against my body, cresting at my midsection. I hesitated and considered turning around. The soles of my feet started to slide and I lost contact with the earth. Now I had no choice but to move forward faster, angling my path down and across, so I could get to the shallows, now just thirty feet across from me. Still angling down and across, I started shuffling my feet along the smooth stones on the bottom until suddenly I stumbled over a large rock and started to swim. *Don't panic*, I thought. *You got this. Keep looking at your target across the river.* I could hear the sucking sound of the rapid below. Water leaked down my legs. Fear enveloped my soul. I had totally misjudged the depth and speed of this section. *Maybe I will reconnect with my grandfather after all!*

Desperately skipping my feet along the floor of the river, trying to regain purchase on the gravel in the accelerating current, I began to paddle with my left arm as water flowed into my waders. As I moved closer to the shallows on the other side, the current suddenly switched off and my feet touched down. The strong current released from my side and I took a deep breath, glad to have made it to the other side. Luckily the air temperature was hot and the amount of water in my waders minimal. I climbed to the bank, elated and invigorated. I sat down to remove the water from my waders and reflected on the magnificence of the canyon.

The Black Canyon of the Gunnison gets its name from the sheer size of the canyon walls that prevent sunlight from penetrating its depths; the canyon is often shrouded in shadow, causing the massive rocks to

appear black. Parts of the canyon have been recorded to have only thir-
ty-three minutes of sun a day. The walls here ascend for thousands of
feet from the bottom of the canyon, making them the tallest sheer cliffs
in Colorado. There are bigger, longer, narrower, and steeper canyons
across the West, but in my experience as a fisherman, none combine
darkness with light, nor dread with joy, quite like the Black Canyon.

I recall one trip that Paul and I took nearby in the Black Canyon
years before when we were in our drug phase, often combining pot,
booze, and other "medicinals" into our fishing ritual. On that particular
occasion we decided to explore another new trail we had never used
to descend to the Gunnison River. Paul and I didn't do a lot of magic
mushrooms together, and perhaps it was only the second or third time
we had done them, but that was the first and last time we tried to fish after taking psilocybin. Coming on to mushrooms shifted my perception
of reality. What I remember most is the way trees become like entities;
they no longer look solid or inanimate. Instead they become transparent and communicative as though their ancientness now speaks. Like
all the objects around me they ripple, shimmer, and breathe as though
they are a part of me and I am a part of them. Certain objects like rocks
glow with halos while others seem to melt into the environment. I've
only taken mushrooms twice while trying to fish and both times I ended
up not fishing at all.

On that particular trip, Paul and I were coming on to the mushrooms when we asked a local hiker to help us find the trail leading
down to the Gunnison River. Paul and I both thought we were listening
to her directions, but as we walked toward the edge of the canyon,
neither of us could remember what she said. "I think this is it," I said
to Paul, convinced that the deer trail I found was the way down. As the
psychedelic effects of the mushrooms strengthened, we climbed deeper
and deeper down the side-canyon, which in turn became steeper and
steeper. I remember feeling like my stomach was full of real butterflies,
likely because I feared losing my life to the canyon.

As we descended, the draw got even steeper. We finally had to take off our backpacks and hand them to one another. Because we were under the influence, neither of us had the sense to perceive the severe danger and understand that we were not following a trail of any kind. It wasn't until we came to a thirty-foot shelf that we realized our foolishness. Resting against a fifty-degree incline behind us, we shuffled to the edge and stared over a 1,500-foot cliff to the river below. "I don't think this is the trail," Paul said. We started laughing. Our fright melted into inane laughter that lasted, on and off, the rest of the afternoon and into the night. Before we left, I looked out over the canyon. Standing there, I recall feeling like there was no difference between me and the canyon: it was part of me and I was part of it. It was as if death was of no concern because Paul, me, the canyon, and everything and everyone were all part of the universe, and nothing could be lost.

While the climb back up was not exactly safe, we made it to the rim, where we pitched our tent, concerned that a park ranger who walked by would turn us in for the amount of uncontrollable laughter she witnessed between us. We laughed, literally, for hours. The next day, our sides ached as though a reminder for how we had tricked death. We admitted how foolish we had been, especially after discovering the actual trail and witnessing how it was as wide as a road. Walking on what felt like a superhighway in comparison made us feel incredulous as to how we could have followed a deer trail, or more like a mountain goat trail, to the edge of a sheer cliff the day before.

When we finally reached the river on that trip (and were no longer tripping), the fishing was decent but nothing to write home about. The fish were relatively small. Looking back, perhaps *everything* else just seemed small because in my mind *everything* was eclipsed by the insanity of our descent the day before and the immensity of *that feeling* that I was one with the canyon.

Splash! A loud slurp slammed me back to the present. I looked up and saw Slide Draw across the river, where we had descended, but I could not find the ripple on the water. I had heard the unmistakable sound of a large feeding trout and my hands started to sweat. Following the shore to the enormous wall in front of me I craned my neck to the sky. Peering up, I could see how this enormous massif cliffed-out, which meant I would not be able to wade any further upstream. I thought to myself that any insects flying on the prevailing winds up the canyon were bound to run into to this wall as well, perhaps stunning the critters long enough to fall into the slow deep water below: perfect big-fish habitat. While I didn't immediately see any fish feeding on the surface, I knew that this was the kind of water where big rainbows live and, more importantly, where they eat. Besides, I had just heard one feed so I knew they were feeding on the surface.

I picked a section below the perfect part of the run, knowing that it was not likely to hold any fish, and I cast my grandfather's rod for the first time. Casting bamboo was clumsy at first and it felt like I had to wait an eternity for the line to turn over properly, my fly line opening up into a much larger loop compared to the tighter loop I was accustomed to with a faster-action graphite rod. The two-inch long Sofa Pillow fly pattern splat on the water even when I tried to land it softly. Instead of rolling out straight, the line piled up like a snake in front of the large fly. My casting form with the bamboo rod was so poor that I reflexively looked over my shoulder to make sure no one had witnessed my ineptitude. Of course, no one was around for miles except Paul, so I laughed loudly in spite of myself. *Paul knew about this spot, and turned me onto it,* I thought. He encouraged me to cross and go upstream. I was certain he planned to fish here, but when he witnessed my meltdown with the rod debacle he must have offered the spot to me as an act of mercy.

I brushed off the doubt by waiting for what felt like an eternity on my back cast, then making the forward cast with less power, stopping abruptly at what would be considered ten o'clock on a watch face. The fly landed with the leader and line straight to the rod without the slack I initially had. "Two o'clock, ten o'clock with a long wait in between…and never rushing the cast," I said again out loud as though coaching myself.

I knew I was casting with a very fickle rod but I'd worked the kinks out and was ready to fish in the sweet spot.

Just before casting to where I suspected a big fish may lie, I stopped momentarily and noticed a fluttering insect, the size of a small bird, slam into the cliff and drop instantly into the water below. The river exploded a full second before the insect hit the water, revealing a big-shouldered bruiser of a rainbow close to two feet in length. It cleared the water and devoured the Salmon Fly.

I gasped. My heart pounded in my chest and my hands began to sweat as I took line out of the reel and tried to breathe past the instant knots in my stomach. I worked line into the jittering rod and false cast several times, feeding more line with every stroke. *Stay cool. He's yours.*

With my left hand I pulled the line down with a hauling motion just before and just after each stroke I made with my grandfather's rod, which I held in my right hand: forward and back, again and again, pulling the line with my left hand, then releasing it into the rod to lengthen the cast with my right. At the last second, I released additional line with my double haul, shooting line and the fly hard against the cliff as the Sofa Pillow bounced off the rock wall and fluttered helplessly to the water's surface. Before the fly even landed, the trout once again leapt from the water and inhaled my fly while airborne. I instinctively pulled back, hooking the fish as the rod doubled over and the large fish jumped.

The fear and promise of a five-pound trout acting like an aquatic version of the Tasmanian Devil electrified my rod that had sat in attics and storerooms for half a century. For a brief moment I thought the bamboo would break. The rod nearly bent in two as the large fish ran into the fast water of the run. I felt the head of the great fish tugging one way then another, transmitting an ancestral vibe through the line into the rod and down into my soul. Over and over, she battled against the line and current in the eddy by the cliff, then circled back into the main current. Three times I was unable to turn her head towards me. The battle lasted for what felt like an eternity when the fish finally gave me her head. As I got her closer to the beach, I noticed a large patch of water splashed up on the dry rock face caused by the large fish jumping when I hooked her. I brought my attention back to the fish, connecting to its ancestry swimming in the depths and I became present again to more than just the fish or the fly. A moment of clarity hit me and I began to notice things more brightly as I brought the fish nearer to shore.

The light from the sun illuminated the walls that surrounded me like rays from heaven, shining intermittent spindles between enormity. As I slid the tired fish up onto a wet piece of sand, I marveled at her beauty. Looking up, I saw that the side of this majestic fish resembled a prism of light in the canyon above me. Like an ethereal rainbow appearing out of nowhere, I manifested this fish on the beach below my feet. Looking between the fish and the sky, I could not decide which was more beautiful, but all at once I felt humbled by grace, there in the bottom of the most breathtaking canyon in the world. I slipped the Sofa Pillow from the side of the fish's mouth, holding her momentarily in my wet hands. She was as huge as the canyon walls, and I didn't want to let go of her, ever.

Looking back, I felt like God at that moment in time, or that God was working through me. I knew I had the power to take this creature's life, and I did not. As she resuscitated herself, gills working smoothly now after a hard fight, I let go.

I remember watching her swim away and disappear into the depths of the river. I felt a sudden sense of loss and sat down on the beach by the rock wall.

I looked at the rod and thought of my grandfather. It had been years since I had thought of him. We used to call him Jelly-bean Judge. He was a kind soul who often drank in the evenings to ease the pain of life, and living with my grandmother, Mama'K, who may not have been the easiest woman to love. Judge and I used to go fishing in the ocean with his friend Bill and catch lingcod and sheepshead. In that moment I missed Judge and all the others in my life who were no longer here: aunts, uncles, brothers, friends, and strangers who had passed on to the other side of the rainbow in the canyon.

In front of me, the landscape looked unearthly, as though all those memories filled the canyon with love. I remembered how I was in Argentina the day that my grandfather died and how my parents did not tell me until I returned several weeks later. They did not want to disturb my trip abroad. The memorial service had come and gone when I arrived home and there was no one for whom to say goodbye. There often never is.

At that moment, I heard a word embedded softly in the constant movement of sound created by the river. It came from the rocks as old as time, whispering, "Acceptance."

Paul and I camped by the river that night. When I told Paul I landed the biggest fish I'd ever caught in the canyon, I left out anything about the metaphysical encounter that I had sensed. There was a sacredness to what had happened that defied communication.

The next day, we hiked out Slide Draw. It seemed to be easier going back up and we speculated that it was due to our packs weighing less. At the top Paul and I drank a couple of cold beers we'd placed in a small cooler and we recounted stories of the great fish we had caught and released. As we drove home, I got a phone call from my mother. My Uncle Lew, whose father-in-law was my grandfather Judge, had died. He had been sick for some time.

There is no logical explanation for how that bamboo rod appeared in my hand on that trip. I distinctly remember checking the tube before I left home but somehow my grandfather's rod showed up in the canyon, I believe it was no mere coincidence that I was in the canyon fishing with my grandfather's rod the day that my Uncle Lew died. I believe that serendipity and coincidence are God's way of remaining anonymous.

> *God, forgive me for doubting Your existence but the rational part of my brain wants me to use IT instead of You to navigate my life. IT says something like "if there were a God He would talk to me and I could hear Him." I have to smile and recognize IT as the voice*

of my own EGO wanting to get rid of the "E" at the beginning and to add a "D" at the end. "Who needs God when You have me?" asks my big fat EGO. God (with a "D" and not the "E"), I recognize Your work in the serendipity and synchronicity of my life. Even when I make "mistakes" it's as though You are preparing me for the inevitability that I will make more! After all, that is how we learn. Thank You for allowing me to see that my imperfections are actually a great gift You have provided me; not only do they remind us to be humble, they remind us that whatever happens is exactly what is supposed to happen. Acceptance! Your will, not mine! If it weren't for my imperfections, and Your anonymity, I would not have come to know You the way I do now. May I always have faith and continue to grow in Your love and wisdom. Amen.

Chasm of Fear

"Our deepest fear is not that we are inadequate. Our deepest fear is that we are powerful beyond measure. It is our Light, not our Darkness, that most frightens us."

—Marianne Williamson

THOUGH I AM DRAWN TO FLY FISHING ON RIVERS BECAUSE OF THE ENERGY that I feel, I would be lying if I didn't include the aspect of challenge; as Scottish author and historian John Buchan puts it, "The charm of fishing is that it is the pursuit of what is elusive but attainable, a perpetual series of occasions for hope." I am in my element when prospecting for that elusive goal which lurks deep inside Western canyons. My soul vibrates at its highest intensity when I am there. As a full-time resident of Los Angeles, I used to joke that when I moved here I left my soul in mountain streams and that I had to travel to these places periodically to step back into my *alma*. I used to wonder if I had left my soul behind in calmer waters each time I came back to the City of Angels, where all the rivers have been eternally damned by so many concrete and asphalt spillways that stretch as far as the eye can see. Traveling to and from a fly-fishing river is a type of pilgrimage for me, and the river like Mecca.

My fiftieth birthday brought on a midlife crisis of sorts. Instead of throwing a big party like my wife did for my fortieth, I traveled solo in my Subaru to Kings Canyon, the deepest canyon in North America, to fish on the Kings River inside Kings Canyon National Park. It had been too long since I went on a solo fishing trip. After spending three years traveling around the world with film crews taping thirty-eight TV shows on the sport, I needed some alone time on my beloved waters. I had never seen the inside of the continent's deepest canyon, and my soul needed rejuvenation.

I camped out that night. The next morning I met my friend and local guide Bernard Yin. I had never fished the Kings before so see-ing the sublime canyon and freestone river that cuts a path between its vaulted cliffs provided a much-needed lift. Intense financial pressure had made my life incredibly difficult the last few months. The Kings River is quite large, draining the high peaks to the east that include Mount Whitney, the highest mountain in the continental United States. Bernard has caught some massive brown trout, some over two feet long, in this magnificent river. In fact, as I pulled the car into the parking lot where we agreed to meet, I looked below the bridge and saw Bernard wading *backward*. I saw the deep bend in his rod and recognized imme-diately that he was fighting a nice-sized fish. I scurried down the bank and helped him to land the fifteen-inch brown trout. It was a positive way to start the day! We left Bernard's Suzuki Jeep in a turnout and began hopscotching with my car, fishing several sections of Bernard's secret spots next to the highway.

Fishing a combination of streamers, nymphs, and dry flies, the day was mediocre at best. I caught a handful of small fish and Bernard also struggled. As the day progressed, I stuck more with weighted nymphs and landed nothing over ten inches but Bernard caught two slightly bigger trout on streamer patterns, which imitate small baitfish. By late afternoon, we chalked off the slow day to weather; it was considerably colder than it had been for weeks. Periods of rain marked the first low pressure system of the year.

At the end of the day, I thanked Bernard for turning me on to such a majestic and powerful river; it was a wonderful birthday present. As he drove away I felt the companionship of the river once more but, for the first time in my life, it was not enough. As I sat down on a boulder at the edge of Yucca Point, I recognized that a deep depression had come over me these last few weeks; I had been agitated since learning that Amazon was planning to come after my company for $60,000 worth of fraudulent charges that had been billed to my account because of a mistake made by our website's coder. It was the last straw in a series of problems that had plagued the multimillion-dollar business, precipitated by the Great Recession. It felt like I had no choice but to fold my company.

The day's fishing had been disappointing and my leg ached from a fall I took. I was not as young as I once was and it showed in my wading and fishing. I walked out to the edge of the cliff and glimpsed down at the river more than a thousand feet below. Encircled by towering mountains, I felt incredibly insignificant. I looked up more than seven thousand feet to the rim of the canyon carved out of granite tens of millions of years ago.

Out of nowhere, I imagined jumping off the cliff. I had done this before in my mind, half-enjoying the adrenaline rush that came with the thought, but with no intent to actually jump. This time was different. I stopped for a moment and considered what it would be like to *really* jump. I felt this intense energy from the canyon daring me to just "end it all." I stepped back from the cliff, frightened by the power of my thoughts.

I don't normally have voices like this in my head, I thought. I looked around the enormous canyon, now barely visible in the moonlight, and the stars that sparkled above. My fear transformed into faith. *I am sitting inside one of the most beautiful and powerful places I have ever witnessed. I just need to trust again.*

Just a few miles to the west stood the world's largest trees—the Giant Sequoias, some as old as three thousand years. Like those towering trees, this massive canyon was a reminder of our impermanence. As my breathing quieted, the sound of crickets blended with the roaring river some thousand feet below. I closed my eyes and started to meditate. My thoughts melted into the landscape. The faint sound of the river below connected me to what followed; I entered *that place* where spirit dwells and the divide between "me" and the world evaporates into nothing and everything at the same time. In this incredible state of bliss, the energy I had felt before returned. A distinctly feminine metaphysical presence made me aware that it was not "I" who wanted to jump and end my life. *She* was asking for me to give to her all my negativity: perhaps she was hunting the "predator" in me—that evil part that is destructive and negative, the part that constantly overthinks and can make life miserable. *That part of you needs to die so that you can truly live. Let it die.*

I remember what Carlos Castaneda, the mystic novelist, said through his shaman character Don Juan: "A hunter leaves very little to chance. I have been trying all along to convince you that you must learn to live in a different way…. I have brought back your old hunter's spirit, perhaps through it you will change…. One day I found out that if I wanted to be a hunter worthy of self-respect I had to change my way of life. I used to whine and complain a great deal (but) all I was left with was my sorrow. [T]hen my good fortune spared me and someone taught me to hunt. And I realized that the way I lived was not worth living…so I changed it."

Standing at the edge of the cliff, I hunted down that sick part of me, and when I released the arrow I watched my negative self fall into the abyss. In an instant I felt enveloped in love and gratitude. The violence in my mind was gone and in its place I felt peace, affection, and tenderness. The feminine energy of the canyon and its beauty had transformed my fear into love. I burst into tears of joy and felt the presence of all those who had gone before…. The universe opened right there in the canyon; *I am no longer outside looking in. A doorway is opening and I am walking through it.*

As I came out of my meditation, I had the distinct feeling that I was in touch with a feminine spirit. Native Americans believe that a continent's highest peaks and deepest canyons are like a collection of geographic penises and vaginas; the biggest mountains carry masculine energy while the deepest canyons are charged with a highly feminine force. This giant canyon was like a universal vagina—a vortex channeling the feminine energy of creation for all things. It was like being reborn through a giant birth canal in the earth. I remember the energy force communicating to me that fear can be transformed into love and that love has the ability to harmonize any differences, melt away any grievances or regrets, and perhaps help us to unveil our immortality. The same energy told me that I needed to foster this new sense of self by helping others to discover this truth—wafting up from the flow of the river—by honoring my true self…by fishing and writing.

As I opened my eyes slowly, the river below was visible in the light of the moon and it called to me as it always does. *If you help me, I will help you. In giving we receive.* At first, I was unsure if what I felt was God's love. I wondered if perhaps lower gods were working through me that evening; how would I know if I were being tricked? God is in all things and I like to believe that his love and grace is one and the same with the power of the canyon. "But ask the beasts…the birds…the earth…and they will teach you…and the fish…will declare to you. Who among all these does not know that the hand of the LORD has done this? In his hand is the life of every living thing and the breath of all mankind." (Job 12:7–10)

I awoke the next morning in a tent on the edge of Kings Canyon. As I yawned and looked outside my tent to the massive mountains that surrounded me, I thought for a moment about *the canyon as vagina.* I started laughing quietly as it dawned on me why I love to fish so much. "Today I am going to descend and ascend the walls of a vagina!" I whispered to myself, grinning.

After breakfast, I hiked two miles and 1,200 feet down to the river below camp. When I reached the bottom of the canyon, I swam across and fished the confluence of a major fork and the main stem of the river. Whereas I caught very small fish the day before, I hooked and landed a half dozen fish up to eighteen inches that morning. When I hooked my biggest rainbow, the only way to land it was to swim the rapids. That decision took faith to overcome the fear of drowning but I trusted in the power of the canyon that surrounded me and eventually landed the strong fish once it had taken me into my backing.

An angler I met on the path was fishing across the river on the main stem. Remarkably, he witnessed my swim and photographed the fish from the other side using a telephoto lens. He sent me the photograph weeks later when I was in the middle of a stressful business deal and the winter rains had started. When I opened the file and saw myself holding that fish in the sunlight of the canyon, that familiar soothing energy instantly flowed through me again. That power is still with me now, as though it traveled across time, through the canyon, past the concrete spillways, beyond the channeled rivers and into my soul: a reminder that we all can experience life through the prism of the river, which has the capacity to transform our fears into love for all things when we allow ourselves to simply get out of the way.

God, remind me that when I get out of my own way I am better able to let You into my life. Protect me, and my loved ones, as we wade through swift waters and vast boulders into the canyon of our destiny. I thank You for mountains, canyons, and living waters. As I play among these gifts, I remember that my soul is ultimately a part of You, and You are in nature reflecting back to me the beauty and balance that is You, in me and in all of us.

Nothing to Prove

"You alone are enough. You have nothing to prove to anyone."

—Maya Angelou

WHEN I WAS FOURTEEN, MY FORTY-FOUR-YEAR-OLD FATHER INVITED ME TO hike to the top of San Gorgonio Mountain, about a two-hour drive south from our house in West LA. The peak rises above the floor of Palm Springs to 11,499 feet above sea level. I don't remember all the details from that eventful day, but I do remember being nervous on the 4:30 a.m. drive. Today, when I know I am doing something exciting in the outdoors the next day, I don't sleep well due to the anticipation. Back then was no different.

I slept for the first part of the drive but as the sun was rising, I woke to the massive peak towering ahead of us.

"What is that weird looking cloud at the top there?" I asked my father.

"That is called a lenticular cloud," my father replied. Being a pilot and officer in the Navy, my dad always knew about the weather. "It means that it's really windy up at the top. Any time you see a cloud like that at the top of a mountain it means there are high winds." To this day I am grateful to my father for showing me how to read different types of clouds to predict the weather.

We hiked long and far that day. I wanted to stop to look out at the incredible views but my dad was impatient to get to the top. For him, everything seemed to be about the goal, not the process. To savor the walk up the mountain was not in his repertoire; we had a goal and that was why we were there. Like a good son I followed his lead, but in the back of my head I told myself that in life I would enjoy the path as much as the peak.

When I was in first grade I drew a picture of my father, and afterwards my teacher asked me about him and wrote what I said below the picture: "My father works hard. When he comes home he likes to drink wine. That's all I know about him." My parents thought it was so funny that they mounted it and put it on the wall of my dad's home office until I became sober at age fifty.

My dad graduated from Berkeley Phi Beta Kappa and went on to Harvard Law School. At one point in his career he became head counsel for the wealthiest man on the planet, J.R. Ludwig. Along this path, my father chose not to be part of a religion but he clearly connected to some kind of higher power that he found in nature. In particular, he championed that cause of preserving wild lands for future generations. He served on many boards including the Natural Resources Defense Council (NRDC) and the Nature Conservancy. Perhaps because of the death of my youngest brother, only a few years before our hike up San Gorgonio, it seemed like my father wanted nothing to do with "God." Ironically, my mother was the one who took us to church when we were younger, but it was my dad who taught me to connect the dots between the natural and spiritual worlds.

We climbed many peaks together over the years and though he's slowed down considerably after turning eighty, my dad has continued to hike long distances. In his younger years, he was extremely goal oriented; *peak-bagging* fit his personality perfectly. Success was always more in the results than the process.

When my dad was eighty-two, he and my mom visited me in Pacific Palisades, where I was living with my wife and two children. There is a small mountain northeast of our house called Goat Peak that we can see from the road at the foot of our driveway. While it is not like hiking to the top of Gorgonio, it is a formidable climb, at 1,725 feet above sea level. The bragging rights include being able to point up to the peak from our driveway and saying, "We climbed that!" We walked down to the base of the driveway and I pointed to the peak in the distance.

"Why don't we leave from here," I suggested, "rather than driving up to a higher spot up the mountain." Always up for a challenge, my dad agreed and we set out.

"It should take us about three hours round trip—maybe four at the most," I said. My dad said he was ready and that he had hiked for seven hours one day earlier that summer. He always brought a pair of hiking sticks that looked like ski poles wherever he went.

It was the day after Thanksgiving, and while the weather had been foggy the day before, this day was clear and hot. As we hiked down Sunset Boulevard and into Temescal Gateway Park, the temperature started to climb. Surprisingly, my thermometer read eighty-five degrees. As we hiked higher into the mountains, the views unfolding all around us towards the ocean to the west, the Malibu mountains to the north, the San Gabriels to the east, and San Gorgonio to our south, I noticed my dad moving slower and that his shirt was becoming damp with sweat.

"It is hot out here," I said, trying to gauge his condition.

"Yes, it is," he replied. I looked at my watch. We were approaching the two-hour mark since leaving the house and still had at least a half hour to the top. My dad turned to me and said, "You go on ahead to the top and I will wait here for you." I was taken aback; I thought my dad would want to make it to the top no matter what, but in an instant I recognized something different in his eyes.

"I have nothing to prove," he said matter-of-factly.

I had set my mind on bagging the peak with my dad like the old days. I was about to let him know that I would go ahead and bag the peak for the two of us while he waited below.

Then, all in a rush, I remembered the promise I had made the day we climbed San Gorgonio. Instead of pushing past him, I swung my fanny pack around and unsnapped it.

"What are you doing?" my dad asked. "Aren't you going to the top?"

"Not without you, Old Man," I answered. "After all, I have nothing to prove either."

Instead of climbing to the top alone, I stayed with my father and talked. I knew that he didn't go to church, and I thought he did not believe in God, but as I told him about the spiritual nature of some of the stories I was writing, he agreed that life had an invisible force behind it that became evident in serendipitous events. "Do you think God is more present in places like canyons and mountains?" I asked my father as we looked out over a canyon called Rustic. He smiled and said, "I do." As we descended into silence, I learned that my dad had grown in his spiritual life, perhaps as a part of growing older. I learned that I had grown too. Perhaps as we hiked our way back down the canyon, my late brothers were walking with us.

God, help me to see that all things pass and that all we have is the moment. Allow me to let go of grasping so that Your will and purpose may take its rightful place.

CHAPTER 2

Addicted to Waters

The Robin Hoods of Guerilla Fishing

"Every act of rebellion expresses a nostalgia for innocence and an appeal to the essence of being."

—Albert Camus

I FIRST RECOGNIZED I HAD A "FISHING PROBLEM" WHEN I WAS EIGHTEEN during a phase called the *Harvest Moon* that takes place each fall. This phase is characterized by an orb-like illusion that makes the moon look enormous as it crests over the mountains and lights up the night sky like a Chinese lantern. When I first began guiding in Aspen in the early eighties, my great friend Paul J (best to keep my brethren anonymous) and I used to spend nights in and around this event, which we called *The Pig Moon,* quietly breaking into private property to fish *Ponds of the Fortunate!* We got very good at what we called *Guerilla Fishing,* so good in fact that the adrenaline rushes that it brought on made regular fly fishing during the day on public water a real letdown. Our friends, particularly the women we dated, became suspicious of Paul and I spending so much time together late at night in the woods, and it wasn't until the movie *Brokeback Mountain* came out decades later that I realized that there really are men who hide behind the beard of fishing. In my case, I loved women and fishing too much to venture into that kind of sexual experimentation. I was too preoccupied with thoughts of big fish in rich people's backyards to notice how Paul J looked in his waders. In fact, I did not notice how *anyone* looked except the fish.

Paul and I dated women but our relationships with them did not last long; moonlit nights would come along, and instead of going out on the town or to the local outdoor concert, we would blow our dates off to go Guerilla Fishing—just Paul J and me on the open road looking for big fish in private ponds. Our love lives suffered but fishing was more important. We had become full-blown fishaholics!

Suspecting that I had somehow slipped over an imaginary line, I looked up the word "addiction" in the dictionary and underlined a specific section: *Classic hallmarks of addiction include impaired control over behavior, preoccupation with behavior, and continued use of that behavior despite consequences, and denial. Habits and patterns associated with addiction are typically characterized by immediate gratification and short-term reward, coupled with delayed deleterious effects or long-term costs. Addictive behavior often requires increasingly larger amounts of whatever the addict needs to achieve the original effects. Symptoms of withdrawal generally include anxiety, irritability, and intense cravings for the behavior.* Because the dictionary's list of symptoms included things I did not have, like hallucinations, headaches, tremors, and nausea, I could say with confidence that I was not a fishing addict. I continued to fish in vagueness regarding my affliction. Denial was bliss.

By the time I was twenty-one, I had become a full-blown fishing-addict-in-denial. Every weekend had to be a more dangerous operation than the last one. Each night we upped the ante. One private reservoir in particular teemed with spawning rainbows near the outlets in the spring, and each night we would don hunting-style camouflage and drive the backroads by the light of the harvest moon—without headlights. We parked Paul's rig behind bushes, hiding it miles from the water, then painted our faces with clay dirt near the side of the road.

It was not uncommon for us to hop the fence onto a long private road, then walk for miles, only to jump in a nearby ditch when we heard the sound of a car or the hint of headlights. Rummaging through underbrush without a flashlight and using only the brightness of the moon to navigate heightened the allure of this stealth mode of fly fishing. At some point in the evening, we would see the armed guard across the lake as he drove his rounds. Uncertain if he could see us standing on the edge of the lake some half-mile away, we always hit the deck and flung ourselves into the underbrush to hide.

This particular body of water was sensational. Every time in the spring, the first to cast would hook-up with a beefy rainbow, some topping six pounds, that fought and jumped as though we were fishing in the Alaskan midnight sun. Paul and I always worried that the guard's truck would appear just as we hooked one of these monsters. We heard about guides who still had scars on their buttocks and we were certain that the guards would hunt us down with their salt rifles after seeing the giant splashes and waves these fish made when they jumped.

To us, this style of Guerilla Fishing was not illegal; we saw ourselves as philanthropic *trainers* descending on these foreign lands like Navy Seals to ensure that the fish in these ponds got enough exercise. Using a French accent, I joked to Paul that we were "doing our duty," a phrase our mentor Georges Odier occasionally employed to describe his sexual exploits with women.

Another favorite exploit of ours was sneaking into a private club down valley. Andy M, Paul J, and I crossed the Roaring Fork River and snuck into one of the club's private ponds one evening to chuck streamers to big brown trout. I hooked one of the longest brown trout I ever landed. It measured twenty-eight inches, but I hooked it in its shoulder. To this day, Andy M has never let me forget that my prized brown trout was foul-hooked *and* poached.

Paul J and I guided that fall. After growing bored with the fact that the guard at Wildcat Reservoir never chased us, we both took note of a small pond up on the Flats. The pond beckoned us from the other side of a tall fence with a small sign that said "No Hunting and Fishing. Trespassers will be Prosecuted."

"Look, Dietsch," Paul said to me as he read from the sign like a fourth grader with dyslexia: "No Hunting and Fishing except for John and Paul, who are gonna rip some lips under the Pig Moon."

The pond itself was small and very close to what looked like a caretaker's unit. We had previously scouted the property just a few days before the Pig Moon, knowing that soon it would be prime time for our lunar ritual.

We sat in Paul's car by the side of the road eating sandwiches and marveling at all the trout heads popping up to eat damselfly adults. "George Manuel says the owners stocked this thing with Eagle Lake strain rainbows," Paul mumbled with a mouthful of salami and Swiss.

"That means they'll fight like a son of bitch," I answered through a mouthful of roast beef and cheddar.

"Looks tricky," Paul said to me later that night over a beer at Little Annie's bar in town. He didn't like the high fence between the caretaker's unit on the one side and our getaway car on the other.

"Yeah, but there are some *huge* heads in the lake in between, dude," I answered. "Definitely worth the risk!" We sketched out our plan on the back of a napkin like two robbers plotting a caper.

Two days later, we spent a few hours tying flies with our friend Jeff P, who I later recognized as having squinty eyes because he was always high (often with Paul and me). We drank Miller High Life, because I think we liked the name, and smoked "Lumbo," which was my nickname for *Colombian,* which has long since been replaced with higher quality marijuana strains anyone over twenty-one can purchase at specialty stores on the Hyman Street Mall. Around midnight of the Pig Moon, we decided to carry out our plans. At the time, driving while buzzed had become part of the routine, and it never crossed our minds that what we were planning to do was illegal or dangerous; it was an essential part of the plan.

We parked fairly close to the front gate of the property in case we needed to make a quick getaway. Already dressed in waders, and with our vests on, we slipped the pre-rigged rods out the back of Paul's yellow Land Rover and began climbing the fence by the front gate.

"Piece of cake," Paul whispered as he jumped down onto the private property on the other side. As I followed and down-climbed on the backside of the fence, next to the stately entry gates, I stumbled and fell to the ground.

"Dietsch!" he yelled. "Keep it down!"

Springing to my feet and brushing off the pain, I followed Paul, who took over like a commando in charge of a platoon. We hunched over while we walked down the cobblestone driveway to a set of reeds by a manicured lawn. Just beyond lay our prize: a small, one-acre, spring-fed pond where someone from New York, LA, Texas, or some other imagined city had spent hundreds of thousands of dollars on creating the perfect fishery for "our pets."

"They need exercise and we're their trainers!" Paul said.

"Check it out," I whispered, pointing to the dark shapes making tapestries across the water. "It is so bright there are shadows on the water!"

As I marveled at the piggish moonlight reflecting on the piggy water, a massive shape poked through the water sucking in an invisible insect and making the sound of a siphoning water pump: "Glump!"

"Moby fucking Dick," I whispered loudly with too much excitement.

"Shh." Paul pointed to the caretaker's unit that hung above us on the edge of the pond like a watchtower, just ninety feet away.

"Come on, let's go take the hogs for a walk under the pig moon," I whispered with the voice of a crazy man as Paul smiled and quietly pulled line out of his stealthy reel. We used special reels for this style of fishing: brands like Lamiglas or Abel that had silent or very quiet retrieves when reeling and playing a fish.

While Paul pulled out line in anticipation of casting to *my* fish, an even bigger trout rose closer to the cabin.

"Dietsch, fish on this side," Paul said as I started to wade into the water.

"I'll be fine," I said, ignoring his comment, as the fish greed enveloped my very soul. During the car ride, Paul and I had agreed that we would fish from the far side to reduce noise, but when I saw that a bunch of big fish were now feeding on the near side closest to the caretaker's unit, I was no longer in control of anything. The fish had my brain.

When I got into position, I took one tug on the line from my reel and stopped.

"Jesus," I heard Paul across the pond, reacting to the loud sound my reel had just made. Not only had I positioned myself directly below the caretaker's unit, I had also brought the wrong reel. This was an old Scientific Angler reel that had the loudest drag noise imaginable.

My heart sank. I had become the enemy.

Faced with a decision over whether to move or not to fish at all, I chose neither; yet another monster-head poked up through the plasma and tempted my fate.

The line screeched out of my reel as I pulled it out and prepared for the cast. Paul silently protested, making obscene contorted faces and waving his arms like a bad pantomime impersonating someone trying to warn his buddy he was about to detonate a trip wire. I sent the line up over my shoulder, then back and forth, quickly letting line into the front and back false-casts as I elongated the strokes to create a tight loop.

Mesmerized with the power generated from this simple motion, I focused it on the ring that still rippled across the water. Guessing that this whale was moving left to right, I let the large moth-looking fly land with an unintentional pop on the surface. The mass below moved quickly away like it was spooked but then stopped, turned back, and engulfed the elk-hair concoction as I set the hook. The *loud* reel sound that ensued echoed off the hills like a metallic noisemaker on New Year's Eve as the Eagle Lake Strain behemoth tail danced towards the reeds. I pulled back hard enough to change her direction but she continued to run, spasmodically plunging down then twisting up as she exploded across the frontier.

I heard a murmur and saw that Paul, who stood across from me on the other side, held a bent rod too. Another splasher joined the party as the lights suddenly went on for real: "Surprise!"

"Shit, the caretaker!" I yelled with a loud whisper, feeling like a monkey holding onto a banana, not wanting to let go but knowing that I would be captured if I did not relent. I guess all those millions of years of "fight or flight" evolution kicked in, but rather than fight, both Paul and I pulled back on our rods and broke our fish off as we started to run. At first it was a quiet hump through the water. As soon as we hit the driveway we broke into a full sprint, our vests clanging and wet boots stomping.

Paul was in front of me, and as though in slow motion I watched him make three clean moves as he jumped up and over the fence like an Olympic pole vaulter. I copied Paul's movements, surprising myself as I felt my body do things it never had. I half-felt the sting of the salt gun burning on my right butt cheek, but by the time I bounded off the top of the fence, it was seconds before I was in Paul's passenger seat. Almost instantly we transformed from fishermen into fugitives on the run, talking loudly in the night, as though we had escaped the clutches of death, speeding down the highway laughing in hysterics.

"Did you hear him running after us?" Paul asked, gasping for air.

"No, I didn't hear shit, but I kept grabbing my ass thinking I was gonna get shot with salt!" I replied, laughing.

"Dietsch, I saw your eyes when the lights came on and they looked like two Pig Moons," Paul said, laughing so hard he was barely able to stay on the road.

Our conversation quickly digressed into whose fish was bigger and what flies they took, but the one thing that remained was joy. Joy for living. For being. For pushing boundaries. For becoming *The Robin Hoods of Guerilla Fishing.* "Steal from the rich, give to the poor," Paul said.

"Teach a lesson to those poor bastards in a rich man's pond," I said with a laugh. "Educate 'em, then release 'em back so the owners can't fool 'em no more!" I continued.

"Mission accomplished—Plan B: LDR!" Paul bantered back like a commander in a debriefing session. "*Long Distance Release!*" We went on like that for what seemed like an eternity.

Nearly four decades later, Paul and I still fish together, but we do it mostly in the warmer summer months and instead of fishing at midnight, we often get up at 4:30 in the morning to have the public water to ourselves. Looking back, I recognize we were not stealing time back then; it was more like a grant given to us by the Big Man behind the Pig Moon, and I am forever grateful for the gift.

Dear God, help me to release the past: All the good and all the bad that ever existed through judgment. Show me how letting go allows me to better connect to Your will and purpose for my life. Help me to share in Your knowledge and insight by surrendering to Your love in the moment. And when we look back at the past with a focus on what has been lost, forgive us our trespasses as we forgive those who trespass against us. Help us to see that "now" is the gem of what we have in the present and the light of Your love in each moment of clarity.

Intervention for a Fly Fishing Junkie

"Addiction is a relationship, a pathological relationship in which obsession replaces people."

—Patrick Carnes

THAT FAMILIAR SMELL AND SOUND. A PUNGENT SWEET SCENT OF THE EARTH released from rain. The melodic tone of the river behind my parents' house. My senses wide open, I stepped out of the car and into the night. I had been driving for nearly fourteen hours straight and it was now three o'clock in the morning *Mountain Time!* The day had started at sunrise on the Pacific Ocean in California, but at the moment I was standing in darkness beneath the stars in the middle of the Rocky Mountains. I could hear that glorious sound that haunts my soul welcoming me back. I heard the river and I was home again.

I started guiding in Aspen in the early eighties. Now, because my "real job" as a TV producer had all but flickered out in Los Angeles, I had come back to the river that spawned my fishing habit. I would be guiding again on these storied waters after a twenty-year respite. I walked down the path behind my parents' house to sleep next to the Roaring Fork River in a yurt that my dad built nearly fifteen years before. The river greeted me like an old friend, its small white waves glistening hello in the moonlight. Once settled, I walked back out to the clearing beneath tall pine trees to the set of six wooden slats pounded into the side of a tree trunk near the riverbank.

51

My little brother Paul and I had originally pounded these same slats into a tree in front of the house where I grew up in California. Seventeen years later, after he passed away, I wandered into the front yard of my old family home in Brentwood and noticed, to my amazement, that the wooden slats he and I had nailed into the tree were still there. We had nailed them into that tree to start a tree house and they had never been taken down: nails bent and old weathered wood like so many crosses nailed to a tree. With the permission of the new owners, I went back a second time with a psychologist and we took the slats off and put them into a box. I wrote a novella about the experience called "Brothers of the Tree." It still sits in a box that I labeled PANDORA.

Now I stood here in the moonlight by the river staring at the remnants of a crude ladder that my brother and I made some forty years ago, just a few months before I had transplanted those same slats to this tree. More recently, I'd had a bronze plaque made which I affixed to the top slat. It read: "Paul Stuart Dietsch 6/23/63–6/10/72." Tinged by grief, I swallowed hard and took a breath. Quiet like the river, I watched the trees blowing gently in the wind and I felt the presence of my brothers. I recalled how an Irish Catholic priest once told me that the spirit of those we love is always with us like a best friend sitting or standing next to us *all the time!*

"We simply need to accept that presence," the priest told me.

Feeling alone and perhaps a little frightened at the gravity of the moment, I looked at the naked slat of wood below the plaque and recalled wanting to make another one for my older brother who passed away.

"Alfred Kresser Dietsch 8/5/56–2/1/94," I repeated out loud.

I thought to myself how I never had the courage to add another plaque. Call it superstition, but I felt that if I were to do that, another member of my family would end up there too.

I said a prayer of gratitude for being here on my favorite river in the world. I felt for a moment that my brothers were with me, if not here in the clearing, then certainly in the melodic chorus of the river or within its whitewater. I remembered how we had spread their ashes high up in the mountains, in a tributary of this very river. I was now surrounded by the light of the moon and as I walked back to the yurt and lay down, I closed my eyes knowing that when I opened them, I might not miss my brothers as much as I did in that moment. I am not certain what really happened when I closed my eyes that night. What followed became a dream.

I said goodbye to my brothers a long time ago but I was not willing to say goodbye to my mother. It had been about a year since she had turned eighty. At that big birthday celebration it was like she was still sixty. Vibrant and full of life, my mother was *The Matriarch*. Friends and family flew in from many parts of the country to celebrate her life, not because it was coming to an end in any way, but because so many people loved her dearly.

The next spring she had become very tired and after a battery of tests her doctors determined that she needed to have her mitral valve replaced, which meant some form of major heart surgery.

Up until the operation she had questioned the need for heart surgery at her age. "Why can't I just live until I die?" she asked with an ironic smile. "Why do they need to fix me now? I have had a wonderful life."

We reminded her that the doctors wanted to fix the valve that was making her tired, but she seemed to know something they did not. *A mother's intuition,* I used to call it. Somewhere in her questioning voice I detected truth. What if her premonition was justified?

I woke up in the yurt and was immediately seized by the storm in my mind. *My mother is an old woman now and we are losing this sacred ground,* I thought. The river in my mind turned into a torrent washing over me like a flash flood! Desperate, I walked out into the filtered moonlight and sat for a long while by the edge of the river, listening quietly, hoping to eventually hear its words again.

While all rivers contain a certain spiritual essence, this particular run of river and its shoreline always felt like anointed waters. When I brought the slats out of the box as a means of letting go of my brothers, I released the pieces of wood into the fast-moving spring runoff. However, I kept six slats, one for each of us: my parents and their four offspring.

When that sick sense inside my stomach reaches up to seize my throat with that familiar feeling of fear that I am going to lose someone or something, the peace of the river helps to ground me. I let my thoughts float down the river like so many pieces of wood, and like a Higher Power, the river helps to absorb my fears.

I reviewed the situation: My mother survived her surgery but had experienced some memory loss and fallen into a deep depression during her recovery. None of her doctors told us how surgery in the heart can cause deep depression. On top of this, she had been having ministrokes. To me, it felt like she was losing her mind. While the land felt like it was part of me, I knew that it wanted me to let it go. But I was not ready to let go of her, or that land by the river.

At the same time, my father had decided that he and my mom needed to move to a warmer climate. The decision was precipitated by a bout of amnesia that occurred when my dad fell on the ice the year before. This land, this piece of water that had become deeply intertwined with my soul, its Gold Medal Trout waters, and decades of wonderful memories, was at risk. Or was it? I consciously shifted my thoughts from what I could lose to what I was grateful for. Recovery taught me this was the best way to find serenity.

I recalled a Lakota Indian saying that away from the river or nature, man's heart becomes hard. I thought about how Native Americans have always known that no one can ever really *own* land. *I know I cannot possess these waters any more than I can control the fate of someone I love.*

As a natal Episcopalian who converted to Catholicism, I know that waters are often considered the holiest element on the planet and with the right blessings provide the means for baptism, anointing, and washing away our sins of conceit and egoistic pursuit. I saw that I was grasping at *things* that come and go, as a saying of my mother's came to mind:

"This too shall pass." Rather than push the sadness away, I accepted its presence; *nothing is like it used to be. The river reminds us that everything is changing all the time.* For the moment my sadness endured but then I thought, *so will I.*

With this acceptance, the thought jumped into the river and floated away like the slats. I was released and all that remained was my now-grounded spirit. It told me that wherever I was, this place would always *be.* And that, somehow, was enough.

I guided for the next month without a day off. The doctors assured us that my mother's erratic heartbeat was not uncommon, but she was becoming more tired and confused. I decided to stay with my sister instead of remaining in the yurt by the river.

Besides, my father and I were not getting along; he feared for my mom's health and felt that my presence in the valley would not be a good thing for her. The resentment toward my father for harboring what felt like jealousy toward me for the close relationship I had with my mother lay like a camouflaged tiger trout beneath the surface.

One night my father, mother, sister, and I sat at the dinner table at my parents' house. Having just finished the meal, my sister decided to stay over in the guest room. She asked me, "Why don't you stay in the yurt tonight?" Before I could answer, my father interrupted and said that I was not welcome to stay on the property.

"Clearly, having your sister and you here at the same time overnight will put too much stress on your mother," he said. My mom was too weak to defuse the situation, a role she had played all too often between my father and me. My fight or flight instinct kicked in. I chose the latter. I stood up abruptly and, rather than directly standing up to my dad, announced, "I'd say this is the perfect time to go fishing!"

Making this announcement and taking this action seemed like a good solution. I often excused myself from the dinner table to fish the evening hatch. I simply walked outside without a fight. *I want no part of this scene. My dad and sister have had their fill of wine.* I walked briskly out of the house and into the cooler evening air. "I can breathe again," I said to myself.

Being with my family was getting tough, like being in a room with an elephant that everyone pretended not to see. My mother was very tired and not thinking or acting like herself. This made my dad uptight. All my life, I felt like he was not very good about expressing emotion with one exception: anger. My perception was always that his generation of men avoided feelings; they just endured. I also attributed his intensity to our Germanic heritage. For my father to show emotions such as grief or resignation over my mother's condition would have been considered weak or sentimental and unacceptable. Perhaps pushing me away was his way of dealing with pain, so I asked myself to detach with love. *I will walk down the path and give this feeling away to the river.*

My dad is having a hard time dealing with my mom's health and he's stressed out.

Don't take it personally, I rationalized. Then my victimhood reappeared. Self-doubt crept in. I felt like I was being kicked out at a time when I wanted to reconnect with my mother and say "goodbye" to this stretch of river. I felt hurt. I was also angry on some level with my father because I did not want him to sell this amazing house with the river frontage. *Besides, why didn't he make more money earlier in his life so we could have held on to this piece of the river?* In this mix of entitlement and self-pity, I was also disappointed in myself that I could not afford to purchase the house to keep it in the family; all these years knowing that I had my own yurt by the river had made living in Los Angeles tolerable. *Now what?*

My pity party dissipated as I approached the river. These waters had a way of soothing my soul, and as I approached the familiar run I wondered if I was *using* the river to take the edge off. *Is the current's energy like that of the muse, or more like the siren's call of an addict seeking refuge in his drug of choice?* I walked gingerly over the rocks and into the edge of the current. "The river is my muse," I whispered out loud, hoping to connect with the part of my soul that seemed to live here. I stood there for a moment thinking about my mom's condition and, like my father, I didn't want to feel these emotions. I gripped the rod harder and stripped out line, letting the warm fuzzy feeling of the river enter my soul like an elixir dripping down the back of my throat.

The coils of line dropped into the water below me and even though I was surrounded by the beauty of crimson buttes in the distance, the winding river that faded into the thickness of pine trees upstream, and the sunlight barely touching the farthest snowcapped peak in the distance, I was only focused on feathers and water. With the innate motion of the cast, I rhythmically moved the rod back and forth from ten to two o'clock on an imaginary clock face, repeatedly, without thought. I took the line up from the river's surface back in through the rod and out across the evening sky in a process that made the whole world disappear. Complete immersion.

The fly landed softly on the current between the fast and slow water and I felt that familiar dry anticipation in my throat, waiting for that jolt of adrenaline to flow through my veins the moment the fish ate the fly and put a bend in my rod, but the fish was not there. I repeated the motion, hands nearly shaking, feet stepping a few feet upstream each time until the fourth cast, when the fly immediately disappeared upon landing. A dull implosion on the surface triggered my response; I set the hook with the vigor of a prizefighter cocking his arm. Within seconds I was locked in on a large fish shooting off into the current. The line zipped from the water by my feet and into the rod as the shouldering fish exploded through the current.

"Yoo-hoo!" I shouted uninhibited, forgetting all that was or that will be. My pain was forgotten. There in the moment it was just me and the fish. For an instant I was transported up and back from earth in a ritual older than time itself, in the midst of an ecstatic battle that no brain surgeon, psychologist, or clinician could aptly describe. *I like this mastery.* After three valiant runs, the stout rainbow made a last-ditch effort, tail dancing just ten feet in front of me, then turned over, breathing hard in water. "I'm pretty good with a rod, but I need three more years before

I can think like a fish," I muttered out loud, repeating Paul Maclean's words in *A River Runs Through It.*

Maybe I am more like Paul Maclean than I want to admit, I thought to myself. *This just never gets old.*

I wanted this to be about the river, but it felt more about *me.* My ego had taken over. I had run away from everything around me, but with this laser-like focus, I felt oddly connected. Like I was in control of this tiny universe; I was the apex predator. I had mastery again.

Maybe this is what it feels like to be God.

As I netted and admired the gorgeous fifteen-inch rainbow, a bright red stripe running the length of its side and leopard-like spots all along its taut body, I knew I could kill it. I had done it before. I looked at it there on its side in the net as the water gently ran through its gills, *this fish trying to breath oxygen through the water,* and I thought to myself, *I can kill you now if I want.* Part of me wanted to. Out of fear and loneliness, part of me wanted to kill everything and everyone right now. I was The Predator for a split second and then thankfully, God's grace returned and I felt the love for the stream, and this place, and my family, and my kids, and my dog, and my dad, and my wife, and my sister, and most of all my mom—the negative floated downriver and I was once again the compassionate fly fisherman. With the slip of two fingers I released the fly from the mouth of the finning fish. *If she could talk she would be saying thank you,* I thought to myself, and perhaps she would look up to the sky and ask, "Why me? Why are you letting me go again? I know I don't deserve this but whatever game this is, I will try harder next time not to take the bait...or the fly, as it were." Without even touching the fish, I flipped the handle and witnessed a rebirth. I let go and the fish was as though it never was.

I want another one.

As I prepared to cast into the ensuing darkness, my phone broke me from the reverie. The screen alerted that it was my sister. Any thought of not taking the call passed by with the current beneath me.

"Hello," I answered.

"John, you need to get up here now," my sister's voice demanded.

"Is everything OK?" I asked, itching to make another cast.

"No. You need to come up here now," she said again in a nagging voice.

"What is this about?" I asked.

"It is about *you*." She slightly slurred her words.

Why did I answer the phone?

"I see," I said instead. The irritation in her voice, and my own shame, melted my courage to say, "Not tonight. I'm fishing."

"I'll be up in five minutes," I replied and hung up the phone.

Four minutes is just enough time to hook and land another nice trout—maybe two, I thought to myself. As if nothing had happened, I went back into my routine: Strip line, false cast, cast, repeat! I could barely make out the Green Drake imitation in the obscurity but instinctively I set the hook. A nice brown trout put a bend in the rod and before I knew it I was catching and releasing another fish.

Looking at my watch I still had another couple of minutes, so on the second cast I repeated the sequence with another nice fish, this time a smaller rainbow. *I can catch and release a half dozen more before nightfall*, I said to myself as I winded the line into the reel. Unsatisfied with the last two fish, I began to walk back up to my parents' house as a familiar feeling of amplified guilt began to pour over me. Negativity crept in like a thief in the night. Walking up the trail, I looked back at the water behind me longingly. *Why do I have to leave the river?* I felt like I was being called into the principal's office to be interrogated.

Once, more than thirty years ago, I had lied to the headmaster of my prep school when he asked if I had been drinking. It was the day before graduation. Walking up the cobblestoned path, I yearned for redemption. *I don't drink anymore but it feels like I am about to get busted again.*

"Just listen to what they have to say, don't get defensive, and be honest," I told myself.

When I arrived at the bench in front of the house, I sat down, quickly took off my wading boots, then walked into the house in stocking feet.

I half expected to face a lynch mob, but everything seemed relatively normal until we all sat in a circle by the fireplace.

"We think you're addicted to fishing," my sister began.

I resisted breaking into laughter. *Duh!* Instead, I girded for the inevitable. No one ever accused me of being an alcoholic but in midlife my addictive fishing pattern became a harbinger of other addictive patterns that were disrupting my life. My business suffered, my marriage threatened to disintegrate, and friendships seemed to evaporate. I never stopped to think that perhaps my spiritual decline was somehow related to my lack of connection with nature. I was always happiest when I lived in the mountains, where I could ski or fish just about every day. Was I suffering from being surrounded by too much concrete and not enough river, or was I a *fishing addict*? Or both?

When I was in my mid-twenties, my sister told me that I needed to move out of Aspen. She said that Aspen was not *The Real World*. The irony is that my sister lived in California at the time and today—at the time of writing this story—*she* calls Aspen home and I live in California! We've switched places!

Sitting on the couch at my parents' house, I remember thinking that I needed to be careful. *"This is not about my fishing,"* I told myself. *"This is about something else."*

What my sister said about me being a fishing addict was predictable, yet at the same time made little sense to me. In fact, it made me defensive. I imagined this must be what it's like for a drug addict or alcoholic in an intervention: the feeling was dreamlike, as though I was somehow disconnected from the reality of what was happening at the moment. Perhaps my sister was upset at the way I had left the dinner table. Perhaps she wanted me to stay, be like a normal brother, and help her transcend my father's fear about my mother's health.

According to addict specialist Dr. Floyd P. Garrett, "As the addictive process claims more of the addict's self and life-world, his addiction becomes his primary relationship to the detriment of all others. Strange as it sounds, to speak of a bottle of alcohol, a drug, a gambling obsession or any other such compulsive behavior as a *love object*, this is precisely what goes on in advanced addictive illness. This means that *in addiction there is* always *infidelity to other love objects* such as spouses and other family—for the very existence of addiction signifies an allegiance that is at best divided and at worst—and more commonly—betrayed. For there comes a stage in every serious addiction when the paramount attachment of the addict is to the addiction itself. Those unfortunates who attempt to preserve a human relationship to individuals in the throes of progressive addiction almost always sense their own secondary "less than" status in relation to the addiction—and despite the addict's passionate and indignant denials of this reality, they are right: *the addict does indeed love his addiction more than he loves them."*

My sister continued, "You leave your wife and family for four to six weeks, stay with me at my place or here with Mom and Dad, and guide and fish every day. It's not healthy. We have been talking at dinner and we think you need help."

Incredible, I thought. My reaction was knee-jerk, my laughter automatic, my anger hidden just below the surface.

"You are joking, right? It's not like it's some secret," I stated in response, hoping to lighten up the situation. The room remained silent and stern.

"So what is this, like an intervention for my fly fishing addiction?" Again, there was only silence.

"It's affecting your marriage, John," my dad said matter-of-factly. I started to feel the hairs on the back of my neck stand up. I had to breathe. I had practiced this in my head. *Don't take the bait. Don't take this personally.*

"You need to get a job," my dad said.

"Not now, Dad. Not after you and Gretchen have been drinking," I said. I couldn't help it. Now I had a target painted on my back.

"Go on," my dad encouraged, sizing up his shot.

"Come on. I have a job. I am guiding here in town."

"Guiding is not a job," my dad said. I was silently reminded that he graduated from Harvard Law School: *arguing with him always ends with a judgment against me.*

"I have work at home. I am writing and developing TV projects," I continued.

"It is not enough," he said.

What I heard was not the word "it." My shame melted the "t" and what I heard was that "I am not enough."

Fish on!

"Whoa…Whoa…." I said, feeling the pit in my stomach like an embedded fishhook.

"What right do you two have to accuse me of bailing on my family?" I asked. "*You* are the one who bailed on your kids, Dad! Work was always more important than your children! You were never there for us!"

He just said, "I am really sorry you feel like that."

Almost immediately, I regretted what I had said, but I was not about to apologize. Looking around the room I knew I had a problem, but it just didn't seem to be *that simple*. In twelve-step programs, addicts with a drug or alcohol addiction lock what they call *the beast* in the closet for good. In programs like Overeaters Anonymous, they take the beast out for a walk three times a day. But for people with afflictions like debt, under-earning, *or perhaps fishing*, the beast of affliction is out of the closet, walking side by side with us, 24/7.

From the outside, putting down the fly rod for good or finding a saner way to engage with my passion has been a lifelong roller coaster ride.

My sister interjected and said something about the pressure I was putting on my wife and how I should be in LA looking for a "real job" that would help support my family (a common theme over the last half-decade of my life, if not longer).

"I think my wife is very supportive of me coming out here and guiding," I said, knowing there was some dishonesty in my statement.

"Look, I know that on some level Mollie would have preferred that I stay home and look for a 'real job' in LA, but what no one sees is that I have generated millions of dollars through my passion of fly fishing and nature. How is that *bad*? I produced the fly fishing scenes in *A River Runs Through It* for Robert Redford for Christ's sake! What *the fuck* are you talking about?"

Then I shouted: "So what if I am a fly fishing addict?"

As Dr. Garrett says, "At this stage of addiction the addict is in fact functionally insane. It is usually quite impossible, even sometimes harmful to attempt to talk him out of his delusions regarding his addiction."

When I imparted this story to my nephew Chris Kresser, who is a leader in the field of ancestral health, he had a very different viewpoint on my need to be on the river. He told me to look up Richard Louv, author of *Last Child in the Woods*. In his book, Louv argues that children and adults suffer from what he calls Nature-Deficit Disorder (NDD). He theorizes that humans have a natural propensity to be in and around nature and that when they are deprived of this connection they can become depressed and afflicted with other negative symptoms. Common sense, on the one hand, but as our society increasingly adopts social media, artificial intelligence, and virtual reality, we are in jeopardy of losing our *experience* of nature: the river, the ocean, and the wild that has been at the core of who we are as human beings for thousands of years. Thankfully, doctors in the medical field have recently started to prescribe "spending time in nature" to their patients based on research that proves that people who spend two hours a week in nature report feeling healthier than people who don't.

To a degree, the decline in people getting out in nature is also evidenced by the decline in fishing licenses. According to the California Sport Fishing League, annual fishing license sales have declined by more than 55 percent since 1980 while California's population has increased by nearly 60 percent. If the current trend continues, the state could experience another 47 percent drop in fishing licenses over the next ten to fifteen years. While this drop is not as severe in other states, it underscores the dramatic decline of humans interacting with nature in a world that is increasingly urban, digital, and artificial. There is a natural state for humanity and it is often found in the stillness of nature.

In psychology, there is a hypothesis called biophilia. The idea is that we are still biologically hunters, fishermen, and gatherers; we need direct involvement in nature. As human beings, we need to see natural shapes in the horizon or in the water and the natural sounds like crickets, birds, and rapids to keep our sanity. When we don't get that, our wellness decreases. While this is still only a hypothesis—at some level we don't fully understand how the human body needs nature—the concept of needing nature interwoven in the fabric of our lives is as ancient as the need to catch a fish for our survival.

I know that I experience a form of depression when I am *not* in and around nature. If I go for long periods of time without standing in water waving my wand, it is really difficult for me to leave once I do get on the water. I know that I am not alone. There are tens of thousands of us who suffer from whatever this affliction is: fishing biophilia, NDD, fishaholism, or whatever you want to call it! We call it *fun*!

While I am not certain if my love of fly fishing is a passion, an obsession, or an addiction, I know that I need it like a flower needs the rain. So the question remains, "Are we talking about showers or a deluge?" In flower-speak, perhaps I am like that rare tropical species at the highest peak in Kauai that requires nearly five hundred inches of annual rainfall!

I scheduled a breakfast with my dad the next day and apologized for what I said about him. I told him how grateful I was for him providing for our family. We found a way to forgive each other. I told him how I had learned that when any of us pointed a finger at him, or anyone else, there were always three or four fingers pointing back at our own selves! We laughed, hugged, and inevitably talked about the next time we might fish together. There was a moment of silence in our reconciliation and I remember listening to the sound of the river below: a vocal reminder of the power of forgiveness.

If I am a fly fishing addict, perhaps my guiding is a form of recovery: helping others to discover the beauty and innate healing nature of waters is part of my giving back. I know that I need to find balance in my life, one that factors in family, friends, *and the river.* I fashion myself as an advocate for the river and the ocean as a place where we can all go to recover a sense of connection that our ancestors want us to understand before we pass on to the river bank on the other side.

On the Roaring Fork, my brothers are physically present in the river, their ashes having been spread in one of its tributaries called Castle Creek. However, I believe there is a metaphysical presence in every river and body of water that speaks to us if we take the time to learn how to listen. These are the words from our ancestors "under the rocks" that Maclean wrote about in *A River Runs Through It.*

I now guide in Colorado every summer as a means of reminding myself of the power of the river and my need to connect with nature and give back so that others might connect with waters, and themselves. Perhaps in the near future I will have the opportunity to be on the water even more. I now trust that I can fish with balance and harmony. The river in me honors the river in you.

> *Today, in the stillness of nature may I discover the nature of oneness. In stillness I find my true self. Today I offer my thoughts to the service of spirit that I find in the presence of waters; I will respect the power of my thoughts and use them wisely.*

Catching a Glimpse

"Afflictions are the steps toward Heaven."

—Elizabeth Ann Seton

ONE LATE AFTERNOON A WEEK OR TWO AFTER MY MOTHER'S EIGHTIETH birthday, I talked with her in our living room above the river. Nearly three months after heart surgery, her condition seemed to have worsened. She shuffled like a ninety-five-year-old woman and often mumbled nonsensically.

"I'm just so tired," she said. "All these drugs and poking and prodding. Why can't we just let nature take its course?"

"What are you saying?" I asked my mother.

"Maybe it's time," she replied.

"It's not time for you to go, Mom," I implored, choking up and giving her a hug. "You're only eighty years old, and before your surgery people thought you were sixty-five!"

"That feels like such a long time ago," she replied quietly. "I just don't know that I can keep going."

"You have to, Mom," I said, tears rolling down my cheeks. "I just think you're depressed. The surgery. Selling the house. The medications. We can help you treat your depression, and you and Dad will find a new place to live."

I helped her to her bedroom, where she lay down to take a nap. I kissed her on the cheek, then decided to take care of my own psyche; I put on my waders and headed down to the river with my fly rod. I

66

fished all my usual places but the river seemed dead. It felt barren and I did not move a fish. Normally, I would have hooked a half dozen fish at dusk but this evening was different. The hatch of insects was nonexistent, like my hope. I stood knee deep in the middle of the river.

"Why?" I asked out loud, looking up to the gathering clouds in the sky above, directing my question to no one in particular. God seemed far away, like a clap of thunder in the distance. The river's current drew tears that began streaming down my cheeks, falling back into the place that made them.

I fell to my knees, the river enveloping me, and directed my hands high overhead. My fly rod protruded to the sky like a scepter to the heavens.

I began to pray out loud: "God, please don't take my mother from this place. Take away our home on the river but don't take her away from us. Not yet. Not now."

I knelt there in the river for what seemed like an eternity, praying for my mother's healing. I prayed that God give her strength and hope. I prayed for a miracle.

I did not catch any fish that night, one of the few times I have come up empty-handed on that stretch of the Roaring Fork. I caught something much bigger though: a renewed sense of hope for myself, my family, and perhaps all of humanity.

We all go by way of the river in the end, out to the ocean of infinity, but after my prayers that evening my mother began surviving one miraculous event after another. Her doctors changed her medication and she quickly improved. Over time her depression wore off. However, she continued to experience losses as many octogenarians do. She developed a severe diverticulum and had to be flown by a flight-for-life helicopter to a Denver hospital. Thankfully, the excessive bleeding stopped by itself before any need for life-saving surgery. Soon after, she fell, broke her hip, and went through partial hip replacement surgery. As if that wasn't enough, a few months later she had an ischemic stroke. She began talking nonsensically and my father recognized the symptoms. He took her to the hospital, where her doctors administered a medication called tissue plasminogen activator (TPA), all within three hours. My father knew that stroke victims needed treatment within three hours, so luckily my mother suffered no neurological or physical deficits.

Remarkably, she is nearly back to her old self today; the vibrant, beautiful soul I knew my whole life returned, a gift for the moment. At age eighty-seven, she still suffers from many of the ailments that elderly people face, but her fortitude has allowed her to return the favor of caring for my father, whose short-term memory is beginning to fade. My parents still live alone, in part because of my mom's ability to be the caretaker she has always been. Eventually, I know my mother will go the way of the river, like all of us, but I think back to those prayers I made in the middle of the Roaring Fork that evening. Thankfully, they were answered.

My parents now live in Carmel Valley, California. They had to sell the house they built by the river in Little Texas. The new owners tore it down and built their dream home. I often guide them now in the summer on the property my parents used to own. I have taught the father and his son how to fish my favorite spots and what patterns to use. The river dictated that it was time to pass my knowledge on to a new family who could experience what I have along its banks. Perhaps some call that a consolation prize, but today I choose gratitude over resentment and the miracle over grievance.

This I have learned from the river: the ebb and the flow, the drought and the flood; I try not to label things good or bad, for only my mind thinks one or the other. When I let go of judgment and notice how the river keeps moving like it always has, whether high volume or low, it teaches me how to better accept life exactly as it is. "I" am not the universal force. In fact, when I am too caught up in the minutiae of my mind, "I" am often unable to *see* the way the river is working in my life.

"Water is fluid, soft, and yielding," wrote Lao Tzu, the *father of Taoism*. "But water will wear away rock, which is rigid and cannot yield. As a rule, whatever is fluid, soft, and yielding will overcome whatever is rigid and hard. This is another paradox: what is soft is strong." The river demonstrates that we can never be who we once were. My tendency is to grasp onto those things I don't want to lose, but standing in a river, or even being near water, reminds me of the strength in letting go of thoughts and emotions over which we are powerless.

Watching the flow of water, I am reminded that in time everything goes the way of the river. As my mother once told me, "This too shall pass."

> *Universal Source, I pray that You help me to find balance in my life; that I might enjoy the fruits of nature as a means to heal my soul, but not as a hiding place of isolation or selfishness; that I might cultivate awareness on the river so that I can share those gifts with others, not in a controlling way, but as a beacon of Your love and forgiveness. Help me to find my purpose in life so that I might be more helpful to others in their search for peace and understanding.*

My Fish is Bigger Than Yours.... Or is It?

"Avoid having your ego so close to your position that when your position falls so does your ego."

—Colin Powell

MEN HAVE A PROPENSITY TO COMPARE SIZE: FISH AS IN ALL THINGS! WOMEN are not immune from this tendency but it might be said that men are most at fault for comparing in this way. In fishing, I have always chuckled at the thought that we perform what we have taught ourselves or been taught, then display our prowess by holding a large object between our legs showing everyone, in photographs or otherwise, just how large our *fish* is!

Fishing can become an affliction in this regard. While there is nothing wrong with striving for success, I have learned from fishing that my ego can quickly take over, causing me to lose connection with my surroundings and others. It takes vigilance to watch how my mind finds reasons to make me better or worse than; this keeps me feeling separated and apart. I find that it is best to be an angler among anglers. If I hire a guide thinking, *I am better than,* I am not teachable. While I have fished waters throughout the world, I recognize that every local fisherman has insight into the quirks of his favorite waters. I used to practically ignore advice. I led with doubt, judgment, and ego, as opposed to faith, discernment, and humility. Today, I try to give local anglers the benefit of the doubt; hopefully I listen without presuming to know more than a person with local knowledge.

Judgment is a tricky business. There have been times when relying on someone else for guidance or information was not the best path. I may try a stretch of water, pattern, or technique that someone else suggests. However, there is nothing that can replace my own intuition. Therein lies the paradox: relying too much on another or not listening to them at all are two untenable approaches. Finding balance and employing discernment is perhaps the most important approach to finding success in any of my pursuits. Staying open-minded is vital for learning and we are always learning, no matter what level of mastery we may have. Similarly, if I go out on the water and miss or break off a fish, I have to watch that negative voice in my head that says *I am less than.* That voice typically sounds something like *You Suck!* That kind of self-doubt or self-pity may seem very different than prideful thinking, but I have learned that self-pity is simply *pride in reverse.* I cannot become the best fisherman I can be when I am so full of self.

Sometimes when I am on the water and cannot get a fish to take my fly I become frustrated. Hopefully I can catch that train of negative thought before it gets to the caboose! I am learning to take myself less seriously: to laugh at the thought that I am a no-good fisherman when the fish aren't biting. I don't have to engage with negative thoughts or feelings. Like meditation, I can choose to let them pass. Although it's comical for an angler with my background to think I don't know what I am doing, it is a precarious edge between this kind of thinking and one that hides my insecurity by posing as some kind of know-it-all infallible angler.

I once went fly fishing with Yvon Chouinard, the founder of Patagonia. I was one of the speakers at the Fly Fishing Conclave that year in Livingston, Montana. I offered to take Yvon out to the stocked ponds we used to capture and transport the giant trout we used in the film *A River Runs Through It.* There was an amazing Damsel fly hatch going off. These massive fish—up to thirty-two inches in length—were taking these hatching insects, that look like mini dragon flies, on the surface. When we arrived at the ponds, we could see large fish slurping the big blue insects on the surface.

I immediately got that familiar addict feeling. My hands started to sweat. I got a hot feeling in my stomach. *Fish greed!* I knew that Yvon was an excellent angler so I didn't want to dote on him like a guide. He had a few nice-looking Damsel adult imitations in his box and, since there were fish rising all over the lake, I suggested that he fish on the opposite shore, where they were most active. While Yvon geared up, I stepped to the edge of the pond and caught two pig rainbows close to thirty inches long on my first two casts. After fishing for a while, Yvon had no luck. To me it looked like he missed a strike or two by not waiting long enough to set the hook. Fish this size tend to take longer to ingest bugs since their large jaws take more time to close. After witnessing this a couple of times, I walked over to talk with him on the opposite bank. I sensed his frustration so I gave him some space and suggested that he wait a little longer before setting the hook since the mouths of these fish were so large. After a tense silence, I walked away and wished I had kept my mouth shut.

I walked about forty feet and got my line out. As I looked down at the coil of line on the shore by my feet, I heard a gulp. Instinctively I shot my line back and then forward through my hands toward the sound *without looking first*. The fly landed where the ring had been. As the leader floated down through the air just above where the fish had fed, I noticed a thin horizontal wake leading to where a dejected Yvon stood. A pile of line lay just in front of him. He let out a moan as the fish he had missed rose and ate my fly.

The eight-pound monster tail danced half a dozen times before I brought it in and let it go.

As I recall, Yvon did not take kindly to my inadvertent snaking of his fish, but we laughed about it nonetheless! Years later, I heard Yvon speak at a presentation where he told us a story about how he slashed the tires of a car, a trick often used by local surfers who want to make a point to a disrespectful visitor at their break. The car in question was owned by a bait fisherman who Yvon observed walking on the other side of the creek with a stringer of cutthroat trout caught in one of Yvon's favorite catch-and-release streams! I talked with Yvon after the presentation and thanked him for sparing the tires on my car the day we fished the Watson pond together!

I would like to say that my reaction to the splash in front of Yvon was a hundred percent instinct, but in reality I was gripped by fish greed; an objective observer might have interpreted that I had encroached on his fishing lie. I could make excuses for my actions, like the fact that by the time Yvon had regrouped for a second cast the fish would have swum away, but I did what I did, and I have had to live with those consequences (aside from landing the fish)!

Yvon and I are still friends and I admire him greatly. A ways back I spoke at the opening of one of his stores. When I have reconnected since then, I smile and remind him I am still working on my fish greed.

The irony is that years before, while on the set, I took famed Olympic sprinter Edwin Moses to that same pond. Edwin had never fly fished before. However, once I taught him how to cast and tied a fly onto his rig, he hooked and landed three of those huge stockers in a row. I knew that Edwin was a prize athlete with incredible dexterity so perhaps I should not have been surprised. Instead, I was taken aback at the envy that welled up inside of me when he landed his third fish in a row, as a beginner, when I had caught none!

They say that every angler goes through phases. First he wants to catch lots of fish, then he wants to catch the biggest fish. The most advanced angler is driven to the water solely by a sense of peace and connection, detached from the results of his endeavors. Depending on the day, I may revert to my old ways, but when I am casting in the sunlight of the spirit, the river, and my soul, is enough.

God, grant me the wisdom to know the difference between fish greed and serenity! And thank You for my tires, which have yet to be slashed! May we all catch the biggest fish of our dreams without substituting the result for the process that includes surrounding ourselves with the beauty of the environment, and the community of people who belong to You. Allow us the wisdom and courage to become better stewards of Your waters.

Surrender to the Temple of Spey

"Many men go fishing all of their lives without knowing that it is not fish they are after."

—Henry David Thoreau

WHEN I WAS TWENTY-TWO YEARS OLD, I WOULD FISH WITH DRY FLIES LATE in the fall on the freestone rivers of Colorado for days without catching any fish. One day, my friend Andy Mill offered to teach me how to fish with nymphs. Andy, who has won the Gold Cup Tarpon Tournament more times than any angler and is considered one of the world's best Tarpon fishermen, was one of my early mentors in the sport. Back in the eighties, learning to nymph-fish was simply a means of becoming a more well-rounded fly fisherman. I had no idea that for some anglers *nymphing* was a bad word!

Nymphing for trout is a technique that imitates the immature larvae of aquatic insects or other subsurface food sources that frequent the river below the surface. I have done most of my fly fishing on the Roaring Fork in Colorado, a haven for a technique called "indicator nymphing" which was developed for Western trout streams, in part, by Chuck Fothergill, who was another of my mentors. The angler casts upstream and across using an indicator that floats on the surface to "indicate" when a fish down below has taken the fly. When the indicator pauses or twitches the angler must strike *immediately* or the fish in question will get away.

Trout decipher what is food and what is not within a millisecond. A twig, pebble, or artificial fly is instantly flushed back out through its gills. In order to hook a fish, the nymph fisherman must set the hook the instant the line pauses. The use of an indicator is the easiest and most obvious way to detect the moment that a fish takes a fly beneath the surface. Compounding the ethics of nymph fishing is the indicator itself. In international fly fishing competition, anglers are not allowed to use an indicator so they must sense the fish below taking the artificial fly by minute movements in the line itself. The technique is often referred to as Czech or Euro nymphing.

While many anglers believe that dry fly fishing was the traditional or original method of fly fishing, the truth is that wet fly fishing was around for centuries before anyone tied on a pattern which floated on the surface with regularity. Whereas wet flies tend to be sparse and attractive works of art, designed to entice a trout to feed because of their motion and color appeal, nymphs are often hyper-realistic imitations of immature aquatic insect larvae or pupa that were originally drab and ugly in appearance.

Traditionalists would say that the only thing that wet fly fishing has in common with nymph fishing is that each discipline targets fish beneath the surface. Traditionally casting a wet fly meant throwing the line "down(stream) and across (the river)." The angler then allowed the fly to sink and sweep across the current imitating anything from a hatching insect to a frightened minnow. Today, the lines are being blurred as many wet fly fishermen use more modern techniques that include casting the flies up(stream) and across and then letting them swing.

In some circles, indicator nymphing is controversial; purists believe that the art of fly fishing lies in the tradition of the cast and that any encumbrance of an indicator or small weight is an affront to tradition. Bottom line: some fly fishermen have a disdain for bait fishermen, and any semblance of bait fishing, or the use of a "bobber and weight" by a nymph fisherman sounds the alarm! The nature of fly casting and presentation methodology may seem esoteric but it does offer a glimpse into the human mind and its attachment to belief systems. To the devotee, where you draw the line in fly fishing technique defines who you are! For more than a century, fly fishermen have debated what is fair and what is not. Nymph fishing, developed around the turn of the twentieth century, was often at the center of the discussion. In his book *Blood Knots*, Luke Jennings describes the raging debate that took place in England, where nymph fishing was denigrated in favor of the more acceptable and traditional form of swinging a wet fly.

On February 10, 1938, with the world poised on the brink of the most destructive war in history, the committee of the Flyfisher's Club called a meeting at their headquarters at 36 Piccadilly, on the corner of Swallow Street. The subsequent debate, attended by the greatest fly fishermen of the day, was probably the most ferocious in the annals of angling. Even a decade later, in the words of H.D. Turing, the editor of *The Salmon and Trout Magazine,* the controversy was still raging, "rising and waning, like a recurrent thunderstorm." The issue, and the official title of the debate, was "Nymph Fishing in Chalk Streams."

According to Jennings, the nymphing debate started back in 1910 when G.E.M. Skues wrote *Minor Tactics of the Chalk Stream.* No one could have predicted that Skues' "minor" tactics of nymph fishing would spark such a major debate.

Chalk streams are wide and shallow streams that flow through chalk hills towards the sea. Because of the filtering effect of the chalk, they are alkaline and clear. There are 210 chalk streams in the world, and 160 of those are in England. They became the testing grounds for most modern fly fishing techniques. Traditionally, anglers on English chalk streams fished downstream with wet flies, so any other form of fishing was considered heretical.

Before the great nymph fishing debate that began in 1910, progressive anglers developed upstream fly casting techniques for flies tied to represent floating insects on the surface. At first this was highly contentious; however, over time, the practice was accepted by most clubs provided that the angler did not blind-fish, meaning that he had to cast to an actively rising fish during a hatch as opposed to blindly casting here and there to elicit a strike. Casting a dry fly "blindly" when trout could not be seen rising was considered poor sportsmanship.

The advent of nymph fishing was a different matter altogether. According to Jennings:

> "(Skues) had occasion to watch fish, that while not rising, were lying high in the water and switching from side to side as if feeding. They were taking nymphs (immature aquatic insects below the surface).... Calculating that trout spent much more time feeding on nymphs than on fully hatched surface flies, Skues set about imitating these elusive creatures. The result was a series of sparsely dressed patterns quite unlike any existing flies."

By 1938, the Flyfisher's Club debate of whether to accept nymph fishing was in full swing (no pun intended). There was never a true victor in the debate, but even today anglers often fall into one of two camps: those who accept and advocate nymphing, and those who don't.

If this debate is indeed a recurring storm, I have been caught in it from time to time myself. My tempests have erupted around the controversy of nymph fishing versus swinging flies for steelhead. While nymph fishing is not the same as throwing dynamite into a pool and scooping the stunned fish into a net, some steelhead fishing traditionalists would have you believe that nymphing for them is tantamount to such an endeavor!

Steelhead are ocean-going rainbow trout. They are genetically identical to resident rainbow trout with one very large difference: Steelhead can swim hundreds of miles through freshwater rivers to the ocean. There, they may keep going for thousands of miles through the seas. One day, a steelhead may be on the other side of the globe when suddenly the fish will turn around and swim back to spawn in the ancestral stream where it was born, sometimes repeating this cycle a half dozen times or more during its lifetime. These powerful fish can grow up to fifty-five pounds or larger. Biologists have tagged these fish in freshwater only to watch their radio signals disappear once they swim below ten thousand feet in the ocean—then reappear a year later when the same fish returns to the continental shelf nearest its ancestral spawning grounds. Steelhead are mythical creatures, and because of this status, traditionalists argue that they should only be approached with a swinging fly!

Today, the "Nymph Fishing in Chalk Streams" debate might be called "Nymph Fishing in Steelhead Rivers"; the latter debate is little more than an extension of the original argument. It centers around whether to present a swinging fly downstream or cast a nymph upstream and let the weight and indicator dead-drift with the current. Nymphing is typically performed with a single-handed rod that is typically seven to nine feet, the same type of rod that is used for dry fly fishing (although rods up to eleven feet are used now in Euro nymphing). Spey casting, on the other hand, while also a form of fly fishing, is performed with a much longer double-handed rod that is usually eleven to fourteen feet, or longer. When executed properly by a master Spey Caster, the motion of a two-handed Spey cast looks effortless and artful.

The Spey cast itself relies on the tension of the water rather than a back cast through the air like conventional fly fishing. The cast itself is based on the same principles as a roll cast where the angler creates an "anchor" with the fly line that requires timing and precision to trigger the release of the forward stroke, shooting the line and the fly great distances without a back cast. Top Spey casters can cast hundreds of feet, often to the far side of a wide river where the fly then sweeps downstream and across the current, enticing a migratory steelhead, Atlantic salmon, or other species to strike. Purists argue that the "only" way to catch an Atlantic salmon or steelhead is by casting the fly *downstream* and sweeping it across the current, whether with a single- or two-handed rod, an argument that harkens back to the original debate in 1938. This "swinging fly" method is the traditional way trout were first caught on a fly rod in the chalk streams of England.

I first learned to fish for steelhead at the turn of this century by using the same nymphing techniques I originally learned with Andy Mill in the early 1980s on the Roaring Fork. The results were no less than stunning. On my first day of steelheading, while hosting one of my TV shows on the Trinity River in Northern California, I landed nearly a dozen of these behemoths using an indicator while dead drifting weighted nymphs. Over the years, certain zealot Spey and swinging fly fishermen disdained my use of nymphs, arguing that since steelhead swam thousands of miles, to unfathomable depths of the oceans, before returning to their home river to spawn, they deserved approach from a "higher place." At first I wasn't sure what the fuss was about, and I resented traditionalists dictating what I should and shouldn't do. However, I was curious so I began experimenting with swinging flies and Spey casting on a number of trips to British Columbia with my friend Paul Kranhold to no avail!

A few years later, while shooting another fly fishing show, my friends and I arrived twenty minutes late at our guide shop in Maupin, Oregon. We met our guide, Travis Johnson, for the first time in front of Deschutes Angler. Travis wore a brown tweed hat indicative of his affiliation with the British form of fly fishing which favors Spey casting. His strong stocky frame that served him as an All-American wrestler and grizzled beard that hid his baby face beneath the motley peach fuzz gave off a bad boy image from the beginning.

"It's 5.29 a.m.," he told us matter-of-factly, forgoing the requisite "hello-my name-is-Travis-Johnson-nice-to-meet-you."

We pulled out and Travis began hauling down the road as the dory hitched to the back fishtailed in the gravel. He was clearly perturbed by our lack of punctuality, noting that most steelhead feed before the sun hits the water.

"We are fourteen minutes behind schedule," he iterated with an agitated tone. After a long silence, I broke the ice and started asking Travis questions. Cameraman Tim Cash began filming from the backseat. Travis, a World Champion Spey caster with casts close to two hundred feet, instantly perked up when talking about the Deschutes River, his beloved steelhead fishery. He had been a guide there for seven years, even after earning an engineering degree. He told me that he was a die-hard Spey fisherman and that he only allowed anglers on his boat to swing flies: "Spey casting—no nymphing." I had never come across a guide, shop, or outfitter that only allowed a certain type of fly fishing. I had been set on nymphing for big steelhead, especially since I had caught three large fish using my single-rod technique the day before.

"I hope to catch a steelhead on a nymph today," I said matter-of-factly. The muscles on Travis' face tensed as though he was physically threatened.

"Not if you're fishing with me," Travis said.

"You're serious?" I asked.

"Damn right. You're not nymph fishing today unless you are fishing for trout, but you're not fishing for trout since you are fishing for steelhead, and since there are steelhead in the system, we're Spey casting for steelhead."

"O-K," I replied slowly, aware that this was all on camera.

"So what do you think of nymphing for steelhead?" I asked him.

He paused for a long, awkward moment and then looked back at the camera lens staring us in the face.

"You sure you want to record this?" he asked with a smirk.

"Yeah, it's fine," I replied, feeling like a fugitive on my own TV show.

He smiled diabolically.

"I would rather jerk off with twenty grit sandpaper than watch a fucking bobber float down the fucking river," he blurted emphatically.

(Later in the edit bay, I was so enamored with the passion and compulsive adoration Travis had for swinging flies that I edited in his now-infamous line into the opening of the episode about him. Because we bleeped his voice and blurred his mouth for two words and a phrase, the network allowed us to broadcast. Even still, we received a variety of hate mail from viewers not pleased with the bleeped-out profanity.) I laughed nervously.

"Really?" I replied. "Why don't you tell me how you really feel?!" I waited awkwardly through a short pause I felt compelled to fill.

"So seeing that I am captive in your truck and soon to be on your boat, I take it that I am swinging flies today with a two-handed rod?"

"Or swinging flies with your one-hander," Travis replied. "You see, if I let you nymph-fish it would be like me condoning your behavior as a pedophile."

"What?" I asked incredulously.

"When the adult steelhead are in the system, and people like you are catching resident trout, which are like juveniles, we call you pedophiles. When you're nymph fishing you catch both, whereas with a Spey Rod you'll only catch steelhead. Well, almost always. Besides, if you want to learn to Spey cast and catch steelhead *the right way,* you have to stick with it and know you can't fall back on something you know!"

"I don't like it," I said out loud, with a pause, fearful that employing a relatively new technique like Spey casting would likely mean *not* holding up any steelhead to the camera. I was resistant to try something new, particularly when I was already a master of another method. Partly from peer pressure but mostly from curiosity, I picked up the Spey Rod and turned to the camera.

"So much for my nymphing," I said with a shrug.

Casting with a Spey rod requires consummate agility and timing. While Travis was cantankerous and rough around the edges, he was an excellent instructor. He explained that casting two-handed fly rods originated in Scotland on the River Spey in the mid-1800s.

"The Spey is a *big* river so the cast was developed for twenty-two-foot double-handed fly rods that could deliver two to three times the distance of a cast using a conventional fly rod. Today, Spey rods are still cast using two hands but the rod lengths are more commonly twelve to fifteen feet in length."

Once the boat was in the water, Travis demonstrated how to cast with a two-handed Spey rod. He said that fly rods were developed such that the rod would be loaded if the angler thrust properly in his back cast, whereas a two-handed rod propels the line using a singular forward motion without the need for a traditional back cast.

"Like a roll cast," I pointed out. Travis rolled his eyes accordingly.

"The Spey caster first lifts the line off the water with the tip of the rod, sweeps the line backward just above the water, and allows just the fly and leader to *anchor* the cast. This means the line is touching the water one to two rod lengths away." Travis showed us how his partial back cast never lifted the entire line up in the air, as in a traditional fly cast. Rather, he formed what is called the *D-Loop*, named for the curving shape of the line between the anchor and the tip of the rod.

Travis demonstrated how to form the *D-Loop* in one graceful, deliberate motion with the rod tip climbing at a forty-five-degree angle above the water. As the *D-Loop* came around, he finished the cast by firing the line forward with a sharp two-handed pull-motion on the handle of the rod, bringing it forcefully into his belly and abruptly stopping the tip, thus flinging an ungodly amount of line across the width of the Deschutes River.

Since first learning to Spey cast with Travis, it has taken me nearly ten years of practice, Spey casting only several days a year, to get the timing good enough to shoot up to sixty feet of running line with little effort. Of course, Travis could shoot nearly two hundred feet if he wanted.

In awe, I quickly forgot about nymphing as I tried to learn the Spey cast.

One of the odd factors of using this sweeping Spey technique is to *let go* of the line when a fish eats the fly, not to flinch or set the hook! Because we aim the Spey cast three-quarters downstream, the fly moves across the current, so when an angler tries to set the hook, he is bound to lose the fish. This is in exact contradiction to other forms of fly fishing, like nymphing, which require immediate resistance, in the form of a strike, when the fish takes the fly.

When Travis first taught me to fish with a Spey rod, he told me to create a small loop in my left hand between the finger on the cork handle and reel (a technique that has since fallen out of favor). The craziest part of the Spey technique for me is this notion of "letting go." When a giant steelhead takes the fly, we are to "give it line" so that the Spey fly will embed securely into the side of its mouth as the "fish turns." This is perhaps one of the most counterintuitive maneuvers I have encountered in all the years I have fished. For the Spey masters, this concept of nonresistance is doctrine.

I did not catch one steelhead that first day fishing with Travis, even though my buddy Pete—a complete novice—caught and landed one. That evening, at the end of what seemed to be my nine-hundredth cast, with my line dangling in the obscurity downstream, it felt as though my line got heavy, like I had snagged a large garbage bag. This was like no fish bite I had ever felt. After a moment of realization, I instinctively jerked the rod tip up and back to set the hook. *Nothing!* I was supposed to keep the rod tip pointed downstream and let the fish take line. Instead, I reacted and tried to set the hook. I stood there in the fading light of the canyon, having fished all day without landing or even playing one steelhead. I later realized that I had caught something far more valuable that day than a steelhead: Humble Pie!

Today I mostly fish for steelhead with a Spey rod, and I have landed over a dozen using this artful and traditional approach. However, I don't choose the Spey rod because I can catch more fish. The Spey rod has become a tool to remind me that life is more about process than results. When I get fed up with this Spey casting *process*, I pick up my nymphing rod again, only to find that hooking and landing a steelhead on a nymph has lost some of its appeal. It is as though I were pursuing *an object* by nymphing, whereas the Spey rod evokes a more soulful endeavor, one that transcends the need for a photo or bragging rights. Over the years, I am softening and seeing that learning new things about myself is more important than getting what I want. Perhaps this insight, that Spey casting is more about *being* on the river than nymphing, is reflected in Deepak Chopra contrasting object-referral to self-referral:

> "Whenever you feel powerless or fearful, it's because you are in a state of object-referral. You define yourself through objects, which include [steelhead], people, situations, titles, possessions, and accomplishments. By their very nature, objects change, so as long as your identity is tied to objects or the opinion of others, your life will feel unstable. In object-referral, you feel good when [you're catching fish using techniques you're familiar with], your investments are appreciating, business is strong, or your romantic partner is happy with you. But when [you get skunked], the market plummets, sales are down, and your relationship is challenged, you feel insecure and worried. Self-referral, in contrast, is identifying with your inner self—the unchanging essence of your soul. In this state (of Spey casting) you have an internal sense of joy regardless of what is happening around you because you aren't identified with transient objects or events. In self-referral, you experience your true being, which doesn't fear any challenge, has respect for all people, and feels beneath no one. Fear drops away and there is no compulsion to control and no struggle for approval or external power. As you experience self-referral, you pierce the mask of illusion that creates separation and fragmentation and know that you are an inextricable part of the field of infinite intelligence."

I believe that the Englishmen in 1938 were debating more than just tradition. There is something about the process we engage in while fishing that informs us about who we are and how we approach things: perhaps this process is more important than the objects we extract from it.

When I go back to the Spey rod, each cast reminds me to be present. When fishing nymphs, I stare incessantly at the indicator or the line. When I Spey cast, I am less focused on any object so I become much more present and immersed in the process.

When swinging the fly with a Spey rod, the key to successfully hooking a steelhead means learning to let go instead of putting resistance on the line when you feel the tug. For most of us, that reaction is counterintuitive. Chopra's idea of *nonresistance* can be applied to this type of Spey fishing.

> "Today I will oppose nothing that occurs…. The soul's approach is not to oppose…. Let the opposition pass…. Either by waiting or surrendering to the obstacle. The essence of this strategy is to put an end to struggle and conflict by allowing spirit to find its own way to the solution. You are not required to be passive, however. You will only find discovery when you refuse to oppose. In many cases a solution will appear as if magically which is a sign that you are learning to act through the level of your soul."

It is a funny thing, but just casting the Spey rod helps to remind me that even if I do hook a steelhead, eventually I will let it go, and I will be back into this casting process again no matter if I catch a fish or not…. That process itself, the Spey cast, helps me to focus less on the object and feel more a part of the river and what Chopra calls "the field of infinite intelligence."

When I go through a long dry spell while fishing I try to be present and stay in the process rather than the result. I still watch my mind drift to doubt, trying to blame myself for something that is beyond my control.

Wanting the object, a fish, to fill the void.

The other day, I meditated before casting and a thought crossed my mind: *If I practice catch and release while Spey casting, isn't the next step fishing without a fly? If I am committed to self-referral, isn't the logical extension for me to fish with a hookless fly?* The thought of letting go completely and never landing a fish became too much. I tried to let the thought go but it kept coming back. I felt lack. The object of all of this is cultivating abundance, but doesn't that mean catching a lot of fish?

Well then perhaps I should fish with dynamite.... Or bait.... Or Nymphs!

When I came out of my meditation, I ceremoniously cut the line and took the fly off the leader on my rod. I walked down to the water and cast without a fly. The opposite of what I thought would happen took place: *It felt as though the desire to catch a fish was more intense than ever before!* It was as though threatening myself with the specter of fishing with a hookless fly, or no fly at all, created an awareness of what I wanted.

The next day, I went down to the beach, tied on a fly, and hunted down my first Corbina of the season. I had been trying to catch one for over a month, fishing at least a few mornings each week. I sight-fished to this Corbina as he searched for sand crabs in mere inches of water. As he approached, I saw him move slightly to the right towards my fly. When I felt a nudge, I used a strip-strike and the fish was on! I normally harvest the first Corbina of the season, but that day I returned her to the ocean.

My meditation about hookless fly fishing actually *increased* my object-referral. I had reverted to a mind-set that was highly reliant on physical outcome. My fly fishing addiction was back. Alive and well!

In the end, I recognize that the path I am on is not linear. There is no "there" or fish of a certain size that will be large enough that I can hang my rod up for good. Fishing is more a teacher of process than a harbinger of results. After all, I am a work in progress and that is why they call it fishing, not catching!

I try not to judge those who fish a certain way, using one technique or another, fly or no fly! I am grateful for any opportunity to learn about myself and my fellow angler on the waters that I fish. I have a lot to learn both from a spiritual and piscatorial point of view. I would like to think I have become more teachable about trying new things and knowing that I don't have to adopt a certain way of fishing for an entire lifetime. Just a day at a time! Perhaps even moment by moment!

Looking back to my days on the Deschutes, I will never forget the first time I hooked and landed a steelhead on a Spey rod. It came after four days and more than thirty hours of Spey casting. I did what I was told to do when the fish tugged on my line at the end of the swing.

I let go.

I did nothing.

I surrendered.

And that magical fish hooked itself with no effort on my part.

".... A sign that you are learning to act through the level of your soul."

It works. It really does!

> *Spirit—help me to let go so that I might open up that connection between You and my soul. When I am in EGO, I Etch God Out. Help me to let go of all the things to which I still cling. Help me to let You replace all my shortcomings so that Your will and purpose may replace them.*

CHAPTER 3

Reading the Water
of Soul

A Pool Called "The Heart"

There are only two ways to live your life. One is as though nothing is a miracle. The other is as though everything is a miracle.

—Albert Einstein

FOLLOWING MY HEART IS A LOT LIKE FOLLOWING A PATH ALONG THE RIVER. When a path follows the river as it flows, I never get lost. I always reach the confluence and eventually home. The same can be said about the path of the heart. At times, the path can seem circuitous, but upon closer examination, it follows the natural path that has laid its course going back thousands if not millions of years.

While a river's path may twist and turn—with certain tributaries that veer off the main artery—there is always a beginning, middle, and end to a journey of the heart. Often times the brain says one thing but when we listen to the heart we often hear the opposite. My heart has an innate ability to learn, remember, and make decisions independent from my rational thinking. This is no longer a feeling that I have. It is being scientifically proven. According to the Noetic scientist Dr. Dominique Surel, "Recent work in the relatively new field of neurocardiology has firmly established that the heart is a sensory organ and an information encoding and processing center, with an extensive intrinsic nervous system that's sufficiently sophisticated to qualify as a heart brain. Its circuitry enables it to learn, remember, and make functional decisions independent of the cranial brain."

In life, as in fishing, we don't always have a road or "river" map to help us make the right decisions. What seems like a straightforward, rational approach can become complicated quickly, especially with affairs of the heart. I have been a creative executive my entire career, with a focus on moving media, but today things feel different. I have this passion to write prose about fishing, where spirit intersects with the physical. I especially want to write for men because I have met so many of us on the river who long for something more than what we think we have at the office, in our family homes, in church, or at the club. So many of us get stuck thinking that the answer is wanting *more* and that the answers are out *there*.

All we have ever wanted is right here inside us. That seems to be the lesson from the river. It asks me to listen to my heart but, like any journey there, I encounter fear. I don't even want to express that here because somewhere along the path when I felt fear, I learned to pretend that I wasn't afraid. The reality is that fear is my greatest teacher. To be a great hunter, I must first learn to recognize fear and be OK with feeling vulnerable! Although my mind tells me that great warriors must not feel or express fear, the truth is that the first precept of becoming a great warrior is honesty.

The fact is I am afraid of writing about fishing for the heart in the river of life. What do I really know about that and what does it mean? Who am I to guide people beyond catching a fish? Perhaps the real question is who am I *not* to?

The river answers me silently, demanding that I wade through my feelings, but today I feel lost. I feel as though there is no water to wade through!

Feelings are not facts.

Today, it feels like I have come to a fork in the river of my soul, and instead of going right, I'm going left. The water in this tributary has all but dried up but I have continued on instead of turning around. I imagine that I have been here in this desolate place long past the time that ordinary anglers would have given up and turned around.

This is the price of risk-taking.

I went with a hunch that I might find a section of never-before-fished water, perhaps a spring that had never been fished deep in these woods. So I took a risk walking up this dried-up streambed hoping to find something undiscovered. Now, I find myself exasperated, thinking that it is time to turn around. And it is a *long* way home.

I have failed.

I have to believe that sometimes we need sadness to know happiness, failure to know success. Must I endure this sense of being lost in order to find myself again?

Addicts, more than others, search for connection.

The river reminds me that we are all connected and that perhaps my addiction to thought has interfered with a connection to a Higher Power that could become my compass: a means of navigation that comes from trusting my intuition just like I have learned to rely on my innate ability to read the water as a fisherman. Even when I blind cast, I sense what is below. Now, I stand in a barren river-scape and "blind casting" has taken on a whole new meaning. I am being asked to cast where there is no water, and where there is no water there can be no fish. Have I lost my mind?

The greatest impediment to success on a river is lack of faith.

If I lack the faith that I have arrived at the right spot, at the right time, with the right tools, and the right frame of mind, the day can quickly fold in on itself. If I don't find good water or get a hook-up within a short period of time I may lose faith. If I miss a fish or break one off at the start, I may begin to doubt myself.

Doubt the doubt!

It feels like a mental bolt has fallen off my mind and into the abyss of the pool; it can send me spinning and before I know it the wheels fall off. When I have lost my faith, it no longer feels like I am on the right path, no matter where I am.

Is the answer that I need to be hooked up on a fish, on every cast, in order to be happy? No. Happiness is the result of a process.

I will stay in the process, not the imagined result!

Some people call it being in the zone, or the moment, or the Zen of fly fishing, but things happen when I don't try as hard to *make* them happen; I take a cue from the river itself and let it happen by going with the flow.

But what do I do when there is no flow that I can see?

Writing this book is a good example of this type of journey. Part of me says to go back to the more *mainstream* waters that I left when I began wading up the tributary of the heart.

Courage is the answer to fear.

In high school, I first read about a Jewish prisoner of war named Viktor E. Frankl. In his famous book, *Man's Search for Meaning*, he expressed that the only reason he survived his ordeal living in a Nazi prison was that he never lost faith amidst all the evil that surrounded him.

Frankl noticed that before prisoners died, they first lost their will to live and their inherent faith in the moment. Their deaths seemed to have more to do with lack of faith than anything else. Frankl observed that their inner spirit seemed to die when they lost hope. On the other hand, spiritual survivors, like Frankl, found solace in the simple gift of life that they had been granted, no matter how oppressed they found themselves in the moment.... Those who died were so fixated on what they did not have any more that their spirit appeared to die first before their bodies gave out; they lost hope. It is with that insight that Frankl later wrote the following:

> "Don't aim at success. The more you aim at it and make it a target, the more you are going to miss it. For success, like happiness, cannot be pursued; it must ensue, and it only does so as the unintended side effect of one's personal dedication to a cause greater than oneself or as the by-product of one's surrender to a person other than oneself. Happiness must happen, and the same holds for success: you have to let it happen by not caring about it. I want you to listen to what your conscience commands you to do and go on to carry it out to the best of your

knowledge. Then you will live to see that in the long-run—in the long-run, I say!—success will follow you precisely because you had forgotten to think about it."

Even when the well appears to have run dry we can be grateful for the day God has given us. It is in this simple realization that we find our will to live not in fear, but in the joy of simply being alive.

Walking along the boulders and crackling brush within the dry streambed, my intellect tells me to turn around but my intuition counters. *Continue navigating this dry riverbed.* Riddled by doubt, I recall what Steven Pressfield wrote in his book *The War of Art*:

> "Self-doubt can be an ally. This is because it serves as an in-dicator of aspiration. It reflects love, love of doing something that we dream of doing, and desire, desire to do it. If you find yourself asking yourself (and your friends), 'Am I a writer? Am I really an artist?' Chances are you are."

As I stand in the dry riverbed in the tributary of my heart, I feel that familiar resistance. I am lost. I feel vulnerable. I stop for a moment, sit on a rock, and close my eyes. I begin to meditate and breath becomes my refuge.

Let go of fear. Ask Him for faith.

I pay attention to the background. I hear the birds and my sealed eyes fill with tears. The tears begin to flow and fill the bedrock. I smell wet grass as the new flow nurtures its growth. And then I am returned to the sound of the river. I have imagined myself in a pool called the heart, and now it manifests.

When I open my eyes, I am stunned to find myself sitting next to the loveliest of trout pools. I notice dimples on the water, look into the currents, and see myself reflected like a mirror of the world. I recall how I awoke from my reverie and followed my heart past the emptiness. I remember the smell of water in the air when I saw the rivulet. The trickle grew to a cascade within a viridescent oasis and I came upon a spring born from tears.

A part of me wants to cast immediately for the sizable trout sipping naturals below the waterfall. Before I cast I will say a prayer of gratitude. I have been delivered somehow to this place I thought I did not deserve.

I hear the river whisper.

Believe in your dreams and keep on believing.

I found an agent. My agent found a publisher. And now I am sharing my little oasis with you.

More God's success than mine!

> *God, I ask to be freed from self-will that I might find a higher connection to guide me today. I am told that I was born sick. My remedy is to find Your healing powers amongst the trees, the rocks, the wind, and the sky. In the warmth of the sun, in the sparkle of the river, or the melody of a sparrow, I seek to find Your message of love and forgiveness. As I cast my line and hunt with the ferocity of a warrior, may You guide my life with the grace and flow of the river as it finds its way back to Mother Ocean. Like the cycle of ancient waters that flow through and around me, falling from the clouds, to the mountains, down the river and into the sea—only to be taken up by the heavens and repeated throughout time, intertwining with our very bodies and carving our soul—may our witness to the roundness of life be a reminder to serve Your purpose and be healed by Your love...so that we might experience the miracle.*

Catching and Releasing the Present

"Every now and again take a good look at something not made with hands—a mountain, a star, the turn of a stream. There will come to you wisdom and patience and solace and, above all, the assurance that you are not alone in the world."

—Sidney Lovett

EVERY MOMENT THAT I BREATHE IN I AM CATCHING THE PRESENT, AND AS I breathe out I am releasing the past. Some like to call it breathing in wellness and exhaling sickness. Others call it good and evil. Some think I am crazy for even trying to define a simple biological function to which they can attach no meaning. Catching and releasing the present with each breath is a practice just as catching and releasing a fish is a technique that can be refined and improved. I practice each with imperfection, although my mind often wishes it were perfect.

Keeping my mind in the present is not always easy. It may wander to the future and generate worry that has no value. Similarly, the past holds little value except to teach learning and "letting go" of mistakes.

More than twenty years ago, I spent a New Year's holiday weekend at a Buddhist retreat center called Green Gulch outside of San Francisco. I wanted to meditate, do some writing, and plan out my goals for the year.

I attended a Dharma talk given by a very well-known monk one evening. After discussing "being present" in our daily lives, he took a few questions. I asked simply, "If we are called to always be in the present, how are we supposed to make our New Year's resolutions?" The entire room erupted into laughter that took me by surprise.

I later recognized that everyone laughed because they could relate, as though this were the bane of human existence. How do we plan for the future if we are always in the present? Conversely, how do we stay in the present if we are always planning for the future? Perhaps one answer for that question pertains to my wife, Mollie.

Mollie is a consummate and skilled planner. I recognize how lucky I am to have surrounded myself with skilled planners at home and in business. I would like to say that I do this so that I can stay in the present while they worry about the future! The truth is that I don't have a natural propensity to plan.

While I can always compare myself to those who seem to have more or better talents, or dwell on how I don't seem to have a certain attribute, why go this route when it inevitably brings suffering? Toxic shame's only outcome is more shame. I endeavor, more and more, to let go of comparing myself to others and instead finding more gratitude for what I have. This also has the added benefit of cultivating compassion.

Some might say this process lowers expectations, but generating gratitude reduces stress and ultimately brings more abundance. Striving to do better is not predicated on beating ourselves up for what went wrong. We can value self-analysis without going overboard while being vigilant to guard against denial. In the end, the only mistake we can make is to not be present, fully present, in whatever it is we choose to do. Mistakes are gifts so why not admit to them and use them as tools to improve?

Luckily, as I have grown in the tradition of prayer and meditation, I am slowly learning to live life more as a meditation itself and less as a frenetic race to go somewhere or get something that may or may not have the value I attribute to it. I will never forget seeing the bumper sticker on a Ferrari for the first time in the eighties that read: "He who dies with the most toys wins." I know what I can't take with me to wherever it is that my Creator has me going. So how much time do I want to spend trying to discover what I can take with me? The Dharma teacher that New Year's Eve in Green Gulch answered me in much the same way.

"I am not certain that I can answer your question about planning," he replied to another round of laughter.

"To tell you the truth, when we meditate and cultivate awareness we are preparing for the future. We are all going somewhere, so isn't this the best way to plan for that future? In the present."

Every breath in. Every breath out.

Each breath with its beginning, middle, and end.

The two most important breaths are our first and last. Each one of the millions of breaths in between are practice.

I watch now as things come and go. I am acutely, if not painfully, aware of *time passing*. Time is the new currency. And so I return to the breath.

I will never forget one moment while meditating more than a decade ago. My four-year-old son instinctively walked into my arms as I sat outside in my backyard. I embraced him and burst into tears of joy. The moment was all the more precious because I recognized that he and I were in a fleeting embrace and that as much as I wanted to hold on to him and to that moment forever, I recognized that God was teaching me how to let go. In fact, my son had already turned fourteen when I first started to write this book. By the time I rewrote it he was eighteen! And by the time I wrote this sentence just before sending the manuscript to the publisher, he was twenty! I blinked and the dream transformed in front of my eyes. There is an unfolding that reveals itself, moment by moment. Paradoxically, it teaches me to accept that I am perfectly imperfect; my imperfection is actually God's perfection.

I long to escape into the depths of the river, to forget about the onslaught of time, but if I go to the river to escape I am defeating the purpose of the practice: catch and release. A few hours ago, while driving down a back road, I turned a corner and was suddenly bumper to bumper with the back of an ambulance. Two paramedics surrounded a gurney while another pumped up and down with her arms, performing CPR on a middle-aged man. I could see his large belly protruding beneath his shirt as two of the paramedics switched places and now a man pumped the dying man's chest. Frozen, I stopped the car and out of instinct I prayed. My hands came together and I asked God to give this man another chance at life. I thought of all the mistakes he made, the people he loved, and the things he tried to achieve. The only thing that stuck was love. I prayed that he had found enough love for himself and others in this life.

As I watched them place his body inside of the ambulance, I thought of the stonefly. *When she crawls out of the river like an armored adventurer, does she think this is the end?* Following an instinct to leave the water and to crawl out of it entirely, I wondered if she feels fear. Does she think she is dying? She must find the courage to leave the only environment, the only home, that she has ever known. She exchanges water for land and H_2O for O_2. Even as she crawls out of the waters she has lived in her whole life, she is literally ready to fly; she is nothing more than a winged creature encased in her old body. She has been preparing her whole life for this moment, whether she has known it or not, and now she will leave her river existence behind, crack through the skin of her old life that now becomes her exoskeleton, and don wings to take flight into a new world she has never experienced: one made of air and not water.

Finding gratitude in each moment is the gift behind each and every pressing thought. It is my key to moving beyond what I perceive as limitations. When each breath becomes a gift, life takes on a transformative quality. All the answers are there in the moment without having to *think* about anything. There is only so much I, my *self*, can do before I must accept the power of something that is beyond *me*. I place my faith in His hands whether I am on the water casting to a fish or in a car witnessing the possible death of a stranger. The river is a temple, and my rod a tool for divining.

Last Ash Wednesday, as I sat in the pews of my church praying, I began to doubt the existence of God. What if I am out on this limb and it breaks? What if this is all that there is?

You must risk failure to find the answers!

In Luke 5:1–11, Jesus is standing by a lake and talking about the word of God when he gets into a boat and starts teaching Simon and the other fishermen about the difference between doubt and faith. When Jesus suggests putting the nets into the water to catch fish, Simon doubts him by saying, *"Master, we've worked hard all night and haven't caught anything. But because you say so, I will let down the nets."* Soon, they end up catching so many fish the nets nearly break and sink the boats. Yet Simon appears to be driven by his shame and disbelief; he chastises himself and says he is unworthy rather than accepting the miracle he has witnessed. Eventually, Simon and three other disciples accept their fate and are converted from ordinary fishermen to fishers of men.

Jesus was the greatest fisherman to walk the earth! He is the embodiment of the divine, a divinity that reflects the boundless and infinite source that is spirit. It is no coincidence that Jesus was an angler; no matter what you believe, there is perhaps no greater metaphor for spirituality than fishing, with its silent promise of reaping unseen reward and a path where courage opens the gate to miracles.

That particular Wednesday in church, I became overwhelmed by the sense that all the humans here at this moment, in the church and elsewhere, would not be walking the planet some day in the future. It was as if all the parishioners became ghost-like creatures walking up and down the aisles.

Instead of sadness, I felt intense joy.

We are all going home to the same place.

Ashes to ashes.

Dust to dust.

Like the stonefly, we too will don wings and learn to fly.

Lord Creator, I pray that You keep those that we love out of harm's way but I know that like the river, there is an ebb and flow. We are here on this earth for a short while. Let Your waters remind us that our spirits will live on forever. Lift us up past our fears like the Great Salmon who navigate Your powerful waterfalls as they make their final journey home. Just as the waters in the great rivers have flowed throughout time, may You grant that our love will grow in You and that our souls may flow out to the sea of eternity—connected by Your peace. Amen.

Forgiveness for the One that Got Away

"The Clouds are rivers that already know the Sea."

—Paulo Coelho

MY TASTE BUDS KNOW THE FLAVOR OF FISH GREED, AND JUST AS I SALIVATE when certain food is put in front of me, I drool when I see a big fat rainbow sipping midges. My palms get sweaty, my heart rate goes up, and I am like a Golden Retriever waiting to fetch the ball. Nothing can get me off my target. In these moments, time has no relevance. In many ways, I love to fish because it gives me a high. When I spy a big rainbow, I can become time-drunk standing in front of Oncorhynchus Mykiss, changing flies one after the other, knowing that he is bound to eat something.

If I could just figure out what he is going to take! In my experience, some fish just won't eat an artificial fly. I have become better at recognizing when one of these fish is a "time waster," but sometimes I just cannot find the strength to give up. Occasionally the extra time and effort pays off and I end up hooking and landing a trophy trout. It is this fleeting success, when I actually make the impossible happen, that fosters my willingness to fail repeatedly. Many anglers have told me, and through experience I have learned, that to catch a large trout on a piece of water like a tail water fishery, an angler sometimes has to change flies more than a dozen times and spend *hours* over one fish. Even in places like New Zealand, where the fish may have never seen a human, I have had to spend long periods of time changing numerous patterns to get a fish to eat. Don't even get me started on steelheading. I have spent ten days Spey casting with a two-handed rod, over and over again, without so much as hooking a fish! Perhaps we do what we do while *fishing* because there is something going on that is more than *catching*.

I have learned more about myself when I have failed than when I have succeeded. The classic phrase, *the one that got away*, says so much about the human mind. We may catch twenty fish one day, but it is the one that got away that we remember. *Why is that?* We can describe in detail how the fish finally took our fly but then promptly broke the line when it jumped into a bush, flopped around on the ground, and then slipped back into the water, never to be seen again. Our mind often remembers the ones that got away more than it remembers the ones we landed, because we become obsessed with what could have been.

And then there's the one that would not eat at all. I can see him and he is feeding, but whatever I throw at him will not work. Most anglers will see a fish working like this, constantly refusing artificials and even some naturals, and move on to search for less finicky fish.

So perhaps I am not *normal!* There seems to be a threshold for me that is higher than the average angler: A tolerance for pain and humiliation that goes beyond the average. All fueled by *sheer will!* And chances are I will fail.

Google CEO Eric Schmidt not only celebrates failure, his company provides employees with bonuses for taking risks that lead to failure. Many analysts agree that Google's success is paradoxical in that it is born from a culture where failure and success are equally valued, especially when developing radical new out-of-the-box technologies like self-driving cars. The company recognizes the need to fail in order to find that needle in the haystack. For decades, Silicon Valley's embracement of failure has been arguably slow in permeating the larger American culture. Sometimes it feels like we are still suffering a hangover from the 1950s, when UCLA Bruins football coach Henry Sanders exclaimed, "Winning isn't everything, it's the only thing." (Many people believe that Vince Lombardi or Paul "Bear" Bryant coined this term, but it was Sanders.) Since then, neuroscience has helped illuminate how this type of fixed mind-set, that shames failure and glorifies success, actually stifles human development. According to Stanford psychologist Carol Dweck, one of the world's leading researchers in the field of motivation, developing a growth mind-set is the antidote to this kind of perfectionist thinking. "People with a growth mind-set are also constantly monitoring what's going on, but their internal monologue is not about judging themselves and others in this way." Instead, people with a growth mind-set are sensitive to both positive and negative information, but according to Dweck, they're more "attuned to its implications for learning and constructive action: What can I learn from this? How can I improve?"

A normal amount of doubt regarding success is usually present in most people. However, when the fear of failure becomes extreme, the medical community calls it atychiphobia. It is no coincidence that perfectionism is often cited as a cause of atychiphobia.

I don't consider myself afflicted by atychiphobia; however, I am all too familiar with the fear of failure and the "need for success." While filming our TV series about guides, I came across a story about a head guide whose clients complained, on several occasions, that he was purposely trying to get them to snag big fish for which they were sight-fishing. It turns out this guide wanted pictures of his clients holding large fish to advertise his prowess so he encouraged them to snag fish instead of hooking them in the mouth. Interestingly, Dweck noticed that people stuck in a fixed mind-set will often resort to cheating as a solution. The head guide in question was eventually fired.

When I get to a place where I know innately that a big fish will not eat, it almost feels like I can take that fish's stubbornness personally! In my head, I become the only human on the planet that can make him eat. I don't like remembering the nine out of ten times that I failed with similar fish. Frustration, anger, impatience, bewilderment, and resignation are all emotions that I don't like to encounter, but with fishing I sometimes get to a place where I can endure these emotions only by forgiving myself and the fish for all our collective imperfections. When shuffling down a steelhead run swinging my fly, I have to remind myself that I am making one cast at a time. When I think of being rejected for an aggregate of nearly two weeks, I simply have to pick up the line and make another cast.

In a perfect world, the fish would eat my fly every cast, so when it does not, I have three choices: (a) get pissed off at myself and/or the fish, (b) go to self-pity and feel like a failure, or (c) go to gratitude and thank the fish for being my teacher. By choosing the latter, which Dweck refers to as growth mind-set, fishing without actually catching the fish is as useful as hooking and landing one. Maybe that is why they call it fishing, not catching!

Unfortunately, I tend to remember the *one* fish that got away or would not take my fly when there are literally thousands of more positive memories from each fishing trip. I know that I am not alone in this regard as just the other day I spoke to a Canadian guide I fished with ten years ago who reminded me of the massive twenty-five-pound-plus steelhead that broke me off when my line wrapped around my neck after making the powerful hookset; he didn't mention the beautiful sunny day or the hundreds of large steelhead his clients had caught since then. He too had my "failure" tattooed to his brain.

If I can remind myself of the lessons I receive when life is not cooperating with my will, perhaps I can tune in to that part of nature that contains the spiritual essence of why we are here. I am not always going to get what I want, no matter how badly I want it. If I am in the result rather than the process the whole time I am on the river, how satisfying can fishing be? Perhaps if I turn it over to that melodic sound of the river I can begin to better notice how the negative ions created by the water's movement and the white noise of the rapids are soothing my soul; I can better see that what is required is not a voice that reminds me that I failed but one that *forgives* me and the world for its imperfections. Then, and only then, I can ask *what am I learning?*

I can take a breath, ask for insight, and when the time is right, I will suit up and show up for the next battle of wits with the wily salmonid and the world at large.

God, allow me to be in acceptance today for all that IS, and not perpetually focused on the past or worried about the future. In being here and now allow me to see that this is where You reside. Bless my successes along the banks, but more so bless my shortcomings. Allow my failures to be devoid of lack and rich with the abundance of potentiality so I can see my mistakes as a means to learn, and a way to grow into a better angler and compassionate being. Thank You for letting the river, with its fish, become my teacher.

The River Patience

"To go fishing is the chance to wash one's soul with pure air, with the rush of the brook, or with the shimmer of sun on blue water. It brings...a mockery of profits and egos, a quieting of hate, a rejoicing that you do not have to decide a darned thing until next week. And it is discipline in the equality of men—for all men are equal before fish."

—Herbert Hoover

I AM ALWAYS AMUSED WHEN PEOPLE TELL ME THAT THEY DON'T HAVE THE patience to fly fish. I smile because I know something that they don't: we are constantly plying the waters of a river called Patience and it is the best teacher in the world.

When someone says they have no patience for fly fishing, they are not saying that they don't have patience with a sport or a place like a river; they are communicating to me that they are impatient with themselves. Having patience with ourselves means having patience with a growing, ever-changing creature whom the river has taken into its midst and whose perfection the river will complete in its own time and way. There is only so much one can do to catch a fish. The rest is in the hands of the river.

In 1992, the year that the film *A River Runs Through It* helped to nearly double the size of fly fishing, throngs of never-ever fly fishermen came to the river expecting to find the same solace and mystery depicted in the film. Instead, many of them encountered a sport that required a tremendous amount of *patience*! Everything from learning how to wade, tie knots, cast, where to look for feeding fish, and heaps and heaps of gear, including leaders and tippets that tangle very easily when the angler in question is a neophyte. Within a few years the industry contracted as many of the curious decided the sport required too steep of a learning curve.

Today, guides practically promise to catch their clients a fish on the first day, a concept that would have Reverend Maclean rolling in his grave; his old-school viewpoint was always that a trout should not be disgraced by being caught by anyone who hadn't learned to fly cast first! Using a guide and getting into trout on the first day is a great way to test the waters; however, becoming an expert fly fisherman takes years of dedication and (there's that word again)…patience!

It took me years to catch my first trout! For whatever reason, my lack of initial success made the conquest all the sweeter. This was after my dad took me to the Orvis fly fishing school in Manchester, Vermont.

For me, there is certainly divinity in a river that reflects a divine spirit. I feel divine every day I slip into her midst. I am attracted to the river like she is the most beautiful creature that has ever lived. I want to be a part of her and long to be in her like a lover. At the same time I fear parts of the river, knowing that her power could take me away with her forever.

Last August I spent every morning meditating on the banks of the Roaring Fork River near Aspen, Colorado. I became very quiet and let the sound of the river come up around me, inside me, over and under me, such that I was no longer whom I thought I was. When I asked the river who I was, She whispered that I was no one and everyone at the very same moment. Later, when I waded up through her spine I asked her who *She* was but inevitably before the answer could come I hooked a fish and forgot to look back.

This is how Norman Maclean described it: "I sat there and forgot and forgot, until what remained was the river that went by and I who watched.... Eventually the watcher joined the river, and there was only one of us. I believe it was the river."

I can meditate on this insight day after day, asking for the river to reveal her secrets to me and to reflect her divinity in my heart. The river is the ultimate paradox: Born millions of years ago, its course often remains relatively unchanged over the millennia, yet the moving river is changing every millisecond. As Maclean wrote, "The river...runs over rocks from the basement of time." Time has a completely different cadence here; some say that time does not exist within the river. It lives and breathes separate and apart from us, yet when we open our soul to her with humility and truthfulness, we are offered her grace. The river forever connects us to an invisible flow that runs throughout our bodies, the earth, and the universe, allowing us to tap into the simple truths of love and tolerance. This, I believe, is the Spirit of the River.

> *God, grant me Your grace that I may make the simple choice to live within the boundaries of patience that the river teaches: through love and tolerance rather than fear and loathing. When I am tempted to act out of fear, help me to pause enough to hear Your voice through the ripples on the water. Even when I am tempted to lose faith based on all the imperfections I see all around and in me, allow me to regain Your power, strength, and hope by experiencing the world through the prism of Your River.*

Persistence and the Catch

"For the supreme test of a fisherman is not how many fish he has caught, not even how he has caught them, but what he has caught when he has caught no fish."

—John H. Bradley

OVER THE YEARS, I HAVE FOUND THAT PERSISTENCE IS THE KEY TO SUCCESS. *But persistence without adapting to changing conditions is pure frustration, much like the proverbial hitting of one's head against the wall repeatedly.* So perhaps the question is: *When do I quit?* Over time, I have developed an intuitive sense for when to persist and when to call it quits, but when in doubt, persistence is the key, provided that I trust my technique, my fly patterns, and the conditions. If I don't have the right pattern, the fish are not feeding, or the conditions have deteriorated, then I am sometimes better off retracting the rod for another day. There are times when the river is simply not being productive. However, nine times out of ten I am either not being observant enough or am likely using a technique or fly that does not warrant the particular circumstances. How many times have I struggled to figure out what was happening on a river without truly observing? If I am in my own mind, struggling to figure out what the fish are eating, I tend not to be as open to what is *really* happening. I find myself in the problem instead of the solution.

To be connected on the river, and to observe what is hatching or not hatching, takes a keen sense of awareness that comes from intuition—perhaps even divine inspiration. Without this, we often become dispirited or even blocked by a process of degeneration that feeds the Gremlin in all of us. According to writer Rick Carson, author of the book *Taming Your Gremlin: A Surprisingly Simple Method for Getting Out of Your Own Way*, Gremlin-taming is a method "for meeting the inner challenge that is inherent in every activity from climbing Mount Everest to getting a good night's sleep. It is…a graceful process for choosing light over darkness, good over evil…or better yet, the true love that sustains you over the fear that can destroy you."

On the water and elsewhere, overcoming fear, frustration, or defeat often requires a higher kind of observation, like a developed form of listening that comes from tapping into a universal source that is bigger than one's individual mind-set. The best anglers, as well as spiritualists, artists, athletes, and businessmen, are highly tuned to their surroundings and often use this form of universal mind to tap into their intuition. This type of process, where we learn how to let go of rational thought, only comes from practice, repeated over and over again much like the fly cast. In fly casting we learn about timing: how to let go of the line at exactly the right time—in much the same way a master learns to let go of rational thought and to play from the heart, to be in the zone, at exactly the right times. This requires repetition and more repetition and even more repetition after that! The Gremlin stands ready to strike any time we allow our thought to be on the result as opposed to staying in the process.

When the fish don't seem to be cooperating, focusing on my breath and trying something new is frequently the best way to tame the Gremlin! This is not a prescription for getting the fish but it is the best way to become more present to any experience on the water, and by staying in the process it often leads to getting what we want most: serenity!

Things start to flow when there is a letting go and the angler is 100 percent *immersed* in the work at hand. Our days on the water are like a blink of the eye; we are completely absorbed in the moment. Perhaps it is the same for anyone who is fully engaged in anything. In his book *The War of Art*, Stephen Pressfield writes:

> It is commonplace among artists and children at play that they're not aware of time or solitude while they're chasing their vision. The hours fly. The sculptress and the tree-climbing tyke both look up blinking when mom calls, "Suppertime!"

For anglers like me this sounds all too familiar! Persistence leads to mastery and to total absorption in the moment: when work becomes play.

One time on the Gunnison River, I was fishing on a hot afternoon when the fish suddenly stopped eating on the surface. Having caught many fish earlier on dry flies, I noticed that the big rainbows were no longer looking up, as though the river gods had flipped a switch! I switched to weighted nymphs to fish them in the deep runs but had no luck whatsoever. Frustrated, I stopped for a moment to try to put it all together. It was windy, just after a torrential downpour from a thunderstorm upstream, and while there were plenty of grasshoppers still flying through the air, the fish were no longer feeding on the surface like they were before the storm. The trout had simply stopped hitting my floating grasshopper. Frustrated by this turn of events, my buddy waved to me from across the river and shrugged his shoulders. He put his hands together against the side of his face, indicating that he was headed for the tent to take a nap.

Now fishless for over an hour, with despair knocking on my door, I entertained the thought of retiring for the day like my friend. I stopped, took a deep breath, and asked for a sign. It did not come right away, but like a bird perched high upon a branch, I looked into the water, then into the sky, and back down into the water again. Then I saw something. It was much smaller than a trout. It was a drowned and twitching grasshopper floating just beneath the surface! I flipped the possibilities in my head like squares on a Rubik's Cube. *The storm above us had drowned a bunch of the grasshoppers so the trout were now feeding on them just beneath the surface.*

I decided to put a little weight above a Dave's Hopper pattern, something I had never tried before. I cast the submerged fly out into the current and let it drift blindly, twitching it at the end of the cast. Bam! A giant twenty-two-inch rainbow grabbed the drowned grasshopper immediately and I was no longer fishless! I caught several fish in a row while my buddy across the river slept!

Persistence and insight, perhaps derived from breath and connected to something higher than our own selves, often results in a new approach that will bring us success, whether we catch the fish or not!

God, when I am frustrated and seem to have run out of answers, help me to persevere, rather than flat-out quit. Let me see things from outside myself and give me Your point of view—through gratitude for what I have as opposed to what is missing—that I might better carry out Your will and purpose. Thank You for allowing me to see that I have enough of everything.

CHAPTER 4

Of Loss, Love, and Obsession

Say That I Kept My Dream

"Say that I starved, that I was lost and weary,
that I was burned and blinded by the desert sun
footsore, thirsty, sick with strange diseases,
lonely and wet and cold, but that I kept my dream!"

—Everett Ruess,
A Vagabond for Beauty

MY BROTHER KRESSER WAS VERY SICK. HIS DOCTORS WERE NO LONGER optimistic about his chances for survival. While he had been given high odds of beating his B-cell lymphoma when first diagnosed, it had now come back with a vengeance. No one would say for sure that he would die, but when he decided not to go forward with plans for a bone marrow transplant, my family and I knew that there was a good chance he would not make it past winter. And now it was the fall.

Inspired by the stories I had been reading about a writer named Everett Ruess, I hatched a plan to escape the confines of my grieving mind by fleeing the City of Angels and driving across the desert to float and fish the Colorado River just above the Grand Canyon in a float tube. Alone!

Ruess was an artistic, adventurous young man who set out alone several times—and at a very young age—to experience the beauty as well as the fury of nature in the American West. As a teenager during the 1930s, he met and discussed art with painter Maynard Dixon and well-known photographers Ansel Adams, Edward Weston, and

117

Dorothea Lange. He was lured by the splendor of Yosemite and the California coast and later by portions of the lonely red rock lands of Utah and Arizona. In November 1934, a twenty-year-old Everett disappeared from the canyon country near Escalante, Utah and was never seen again. Although his burros were found near his camp, his fate remains a mystery.

A River Runs Through It had premiered the year before. When I watched a rough cut of the film, I was floored by the emotions that stirred inside me; though I had read the book and screenplay many times, it felt personal when the main character's brother named Paul dies at the end of the film. I had lost my own younger brother Paul when I was eleven. It was the first time, as a grown man, that a piece of art had so touched my heart. There was no question that my working on this film was meant to be. I went home and cried alone for what seemed like hours. Now, a year after the film's premiere, my older brother was dying.

Like Everett, the canyons called to me. I researched the weather patterns over the next couple of weeks and packed up for Lee's Ferry, outside of Page, Arizona, to fish the Colorado River in the canyon below Glen Canyon Dam.

Los Angeles, with its fast pace and incessant demand for material thinking, ground down my soul; I contemplated life without brothers. A drive through the desert and fishing the canyon alone would do me some good. I threw together my fly fishing gear, a tent, food, water bottles, a ground pad, a sleeping bag, a writing tablet, and pen, then headed out on Interstate 15 through the desert with my float tube.

I have always held some indifference towards the desert. In the past, I had done little more than bide my time while driving through arid landscapes on my way to verdant mountain biomes. There was a desolation there that always prompted me to discount her beauty, much like a teenager ignoring the wisdom of his elders. Rarely had the desert been the final destination for one of my sojourns. Rather than being present to its beauty and starkness, I treated it like an environment I had to tolerate in order to get where I wanted to go. Driving that day through arid landscapes and disconsolate horizons, I made peace with the desert and it became my brother.

I drove eight hours straight and arrived at Lee's Ferry near midnight. I stayed in the cabins owned by my friends, Terry Gunn and his wife, Wendy. The next morning, I ate breakfast with them and told them of my plan to float the Colorado from Glen Canyon Dam alone in my float tube. Terry looked at his wife then at me and laughed.

"I don't think I have heard of anyone doing that before," Terry said with a strange look on his face.

"You don't think it's smart?" I asked.

"Figures that *you*, of all people, would want to do *that*!" Terry said, avoiding my question, then wishing me luck.

Lee's Ferry, Arizona is a tiny town that sits in between Glen Canyon to the east and Marble Canyon to the west, just a few hundred feet above the Colorado River. At the time, the "town" was only Terry's Inn and another establishment across the street. Glen Canyon Dam straddles the river upstream, just fifteen miles to the east. While Lee's Ferry and Glen Canyon do not have the acclaim of Marble Canyon or the Grand Canyon downstream, this section of the Colorado River is stunning, sitting below the famous Vermilion Cliffs, with relatively easy access to an impressive trout fishery.

Pulling into the near-empty parking lot by the massive Colorado River, I parked and started packing up my float tube with food and camping equipment, including my sleeping bag that I stored in a dry bag. Since there was no rain in the forecast I decided I would sleep outside under the stars. Besides, there would be no room for a tent on my float tube! Since this stretch of the Colorado is all catch and release, I brought all my own food.

I must have been quite a sight in my belted chest waders with my dry bag on my shoulders while dragging my float tube up to the dock. Six giant motorized rafts bobbed with the ebb and flow of the slow-moving river, with about as many guides milling around getting ready to shove off. I immediately recognized that there were several types of rafts. Some were large pontoon boats capable of carrying up to twenty passengers *downstream* through the Grand Canyon. Others were small sixteen-foot paddle boats with oar locks for noncommercial trips going the same direction, piled high with gear since they take up to three weeks to make the same trip to Lake Mead some 280 miles to the west.

Lee's Ferry is also where the outfitters store their thirty-foot rafts. Each morning, their captains drive empty boats sixteen miles upstream to the base of Glen Canyon Dam to pick up loads of tourists waiting to float down the Colorado on a one-day trip. My crazy plan was to give one of these boat drivers a twenty-dollar bill to hitch a ride in one of their empty rafts so they could drop me off just below the dam, where I would deploy my float tube.

A float tube consists of a customized canvas design that sits over a truck-tire inner tube. It includes pockets, compartments, and a back-rest. It also provides a seat that straddles the inside of the tube so you can sit within the apparatus and use your legs, fitted with fins, to steer and propel the craft through the water. Float tubes are made for lakes. They are *not* designed for river use. I looked at the bright red words printed in large bold letters on the watercraft: WARNING: DO NOT USE THIS IN MOVING WATER! While the words spelled out one thing, I felt like I was reading braille and this was my interpretation: RISK YOUR LIFE TODAY! IT MAKES YOU FEEL MORE ALIVE ESPECIALLY IF YOUR BROTHER IS DYING!

Floating Glen Canyon in a float tube was novel back then and as far as I know I was the first person to do it solo or otherwise. Even the guides thought I was a little nuts taking this small personal watercraft out on the mighty Colorado River alone. Granted, there were no real rapids to speak of in this section, but the sheer size of the river creates massive eddies and whirlpools that can easily flip and drown you if you don't swim free.

Today, this section of the Colorado River from Glen Canyon Dam to Lee's Ferry (and through most of the Grand Canyon for that matter) is considered a tailwater fishery. A tailwater refers to the outflow from large dams, where colder water stored at the bottom of the reservoir near the outlet creates a constant cold-water flow. This, combined with the relatively silt-free nature of the outflow, creates ideal conditions for cold-water fish such as trout once they are introduced.

This section of the Colorado River was originally a warm water fishery containing native desert species like sucker, dace, and chub. Once this dam was completed in 1966, this "tailwater" section of the Colorado became a world-class trout fishery with the help of biologists who introduced salmonids. While the introduction of non-native trout species has irked environmentalists for decades, this stretch of canyon is like the eighth wonder of the world for anglers like me! While the dam regulated potentially destructive Spring runoff, this three-hundred-foot monstrosity created the massive artificial reservoir called Lake Powell that destroyed the upper section of Glen Canyon, said to have rivaled sections of the Grand Canyon. For me, fishing below the dam is always bittersweet. Sweet because we can now fish for trout in this spectacular river canyon, and bitter because of what we had to destroy above the dam to create this fishery. Trout fishing in this section of the Colorado is a man-made phenomenon surrounded by one of nature's purest creations: Glen Canyon and the Vermilion Cliffs.

I had kayaked and fished parts of the Grand Canyon years before and floated Glen Canyon several times with Terry and my friends in a boat. I felt I was equipped to solo one of the first float tube trips through Glen Canyon. My brother was in a hospital bed at Stanford and he probably would never be able to do something like this again, so in my mind this was a tribute to him. Like Everett Ruess, I now longed for the solitude of a desert canyon. My brother seemed to be preparing for his death and I needed to prepare to say goodbye.

I began thinking that religion, like this trout fishery, is man-made and that spirit, like the canyon, is God-made. The two can coexist, just like trout fishing and the canyon itself: a mix of two forms of nature where one is created through man acting as an intermediary and the other through God's direct hand. Here in the confines of the canyon I had come to meet my Maker one on one with no intermediaries. I wanted to know why He was taking my last brother.

On the dock, the first guide I spoke with agreed to give me a ride upriver, more out of a sense of shared adventure than the twenty-dollar bill I gave him. As we roared up the river, the loud twin motors blaring over silence, I craned my neck to stare at the canyon walls that rose up all around us for thousands of feet. It seemed as if the hand of God had painted crimson, pink, red, white, and yellow shades on this canvas of timeless rock. Mornings were especially beautiful here as the sunlight first filters through the steep cathedral-like cliffs, monochromatic shadows mixing in with the reddish coloration of basalt. Before the sun's rays warmed up the canyon it was *cold*, and the wind chill created by the speed of the raft speeding upstream made it even colder! Rime ice bordered the river on each side. I was bundled in every scrap of clothing I had: two turtlenecks, a vest, and a parka, as well as a wool cap and gloves. *Serves me right living in a warm climate like Southern California,* I thought.

As my eyes moved down from the natural cliffs to the man-altered river, I noticed white sandy beaches and long perfect runs. In several places, small creeks entered from side canyons and giant pools were mixed in with riffles and shoals full of seams sure to hold big rainbow trout! My heart pounded with anticipation and I smiled. Man-altered or not, I was in my element again.

Once we arrived at the base of the dam, the driver stopped and we began to drift with the current. I deployed the float tube off the side of the boat. Being a part-time angler himself, the driver wished me luck and, being a boater, he implored me to be safe. I nodded, put my special fins over my wading boots, and as he held the float tube in the water against the side of the raft, I slid into my belly boat, thanked him, and waved goodbye. I was on my own!

I planned to use the belly boat to access the beaches and shoals that straddled some of the best-looking water anywhere in the West.

The river twisted and turned, forming runs below sand bars that were perfect for fly fishing. The average size trout here is fourteen to sixteen inches but some are significantly larger. In many places you can clearly see the trout when the sun is overhead. Many people consider this section of the Colorado to be akin to a massive spring creek but really it is just a gigantic tailwater fishery formed by the enormous Glen Canyon Dam. Just as famous tailwaters like the Frying Pan, The Green, The Big Horn, and San Juan can be fished effectively with scuds, worms, sow buds, and egg patterns, the Colorado is no different. However, it typically requires a considerably longer cast than the other tailwaters (similar to fishing the Missouri River in Montana).

Looking back, I did not notice how the canyon waters seemed to absorb my pain; I was simply immersed in my passion and for the time being nothing else mattered! I floated down to a run below the dam where the fishing was typically best. I wanted to get away from the four-hundred-foot concrete monstrosity that filled the sky above me and reminded me that the river I was floating in was man-made. I tried fishing from the tube as I floated, but I much preferred to find a sandy beach where I could stand in waters and connect with the grounding spirit of this place.

After floating for about a mile with no mishaps, I pulled up to a beautiful long beach on a corner that created a long shallow run. As I punched through an eddy wall, the downstream front side of the tube nearly submerged completely underwater and I had to kick furiously to remain upright. For a moment I thought I would swim but within seconds my craft stabilized, the current slowed to a stop, and I gently found terra firma. Terry had shown me how these runs could be incredibly productive with a fly rod and two nymphs ten to fifteen feet beneath a yarn indicator, not dissimilar to the way I learned to fish and guide in Aspen, Colorado.

I got out of the boat and stopped. The sound of the river filled the warming air that smelled sweet with the promise of the day. I thought for a moment about the fact that I had not yet stopped to just "be." I was so focused on "getting there" that even when I was "here" I almost forgot to listen.

On top of the gurgling rush of the river I could hear swallows and waterfowl chirping all around me. The quiet here was full of life but my mind was full of thought. Even the smell of sage wafting in the air reminded me of my brother, who had become accustomed to burning the medicinal plant next to his bed day and night.

I thought to myself, *My brother is still here on the planet and I will be seeing him in a few days when I leave the canyon.* Knowing that I could still see him, hug him, and talk to him seemed to make such a big difference, but for the moment I was in the canyon trying to forget where he was.

A silver flash broke me from my reverie. *They're starting to feed*, I thought. I began casting and almost immediately hooking fish. I must have hooked, landed, and released three or four nice-sized rainbows when I noticed a submarine-looking shape just below the sandbar. I quickly walked over and positioned myself just across from where I could see its shape. I watched as the object moved over to eat something floating down—giving itself away as a target in the process. I took out forty feet of line from my reel, placed the line next to my boots on the sand, and entered the water up to my ankles. I detached the bottom fly, a sow bug, from the cork where I had stored it, then began false casting, slowly at first with short strokes. With each stroke, I allowed the line to plop into the water directly downstream from me, then I would cock the rod back and fire a cast upstream, repeatedly. One of my mentors, Georges Odier, used to call this the *Leisenring Lift.*

I allowed line to slip through my fingers into the back cast, then into the front cast, back and forth, the strokes coming at increasingly longer intervals as I had to wait for the line to unfurl and land in the front, then again in the back, continuing the process for four or five cycles until I pivoted and shot the remaining amount of line diagonally towards the run.

The fly line shot the leader, yarn indicator, small weights and flies out into the middle of the current, playing out with a slight curve as planned. I immediately took line in through my index finger to get the slack out. The indicator drifted through a deep section of the run, right where I had seen the flash, but it failed to move. Part of me sighed relief as I lifted the rod slightly, ready to cast again. I never like hooking a fish on the first cast anyway: bad luck!

After casting like that several more times, I noticed that the big fish was no longer visible. I never saw him spook but after a few casts I realized that he was either camouflaged or had moved to a new spot to feed. I cast for twenty minutes with no luck and finally gave up fishing the shelf. I instead scanned the water and noticed a section of deeper water off to the side near the spot where I had beached the belly boat. I took the opportunity to switch flies and tied on an egg pattern and a San Juan worm. I knew that in some circles this was looked down upon as a "lower form" of fly fishing. While fishing with dry flies during this time of day at this time of year would have been futile, there were purists who would scoff at me using a "worm" and an "egg" pattern while employing a "bobber" and tiny weights. Any judgment quickly dissolved into the waters of the canyon. I made the same cast as before. As soon as I mended the line, the indicator disappeared beneath the surface and I set the hook. The feeling of a heavy fish was unmistakable!

Her weight, along with the current, put a deep bend in my rod, and I sensed that a big run was imminent. In anticipation, I quickly adjusted the drag on the reel just as the fish bolted for heavy water. I let go of the drag ring as the reel took off spinning. Just as suddenly, the line stopped in the current and began shuttering as though thousands of pounds of pressure were being applied to it. I stopped too. I knew I was hooked up even though I could not see anything swimming. I could *feel* the connection. *I have been fishing my whole life,* I thought. *Of course I know there is a fish on my line because I can feel it. So where does my doubt originate?* As a guide, how many anglers had I fished with who had no faith that what they were feeling was the *fact* that they were connected to a fish? "How do I know it's not a rock?" they would often ask. Of course, when they brought the fish in and landed it, there was now proof that the fish had been on the whole time.

If there were a God then my brother would not be dying, I thought. *All would be perfect, but it is not.*

Just as I had this thought, I also noticed that the fish on my line was no longer moving. I applied a little more pressure but he just sat at the bottom of the water. He did not budge. I put more and more pressure on him and started thinking that I had hooked into something enormous, beyond imagination. For the next few minutes I wrenched my arm, employing every trick in the book to move this beast from the immense current without breaking it off.

With the amount of pressure I have on my rod, the fish would have to be more than twenty pounds, I thought. As far as I knew there were no big browns to speak of in this section of the Colorado, nor did rainbows get that big in here.

"What is going on?" I asked out loud.

"Maybe the fish got snagged," I answered, as though I was someone else.

There was too much current to give the fish line to swim out. The torrent pulled the line downward into what I imagined was a dark and foreboding place full of snags and obstacles.

After another few minutes of futile manipulation, I pointed the rod at what I now imagined was a snag and pulled back. Nothing. I worked it back harder and "snap." The line broke and the pressure released from the reel. The leader flew up into the wind as though in slow motion. Grabbing the line, I recognized that my entire rig had disappeared. As I backed out of the river, one step at a time, I felt an intense anger.

Maybe that was a snag all along, I thought, like a neophyte. *Maybe I never even hooked a fish at all.*

Then I *remembered* the way I felt when the fish took the fly and how I had set the hook, and after a moment how it had run to the middle of the current. I took a deep breath and looked up to the passing clouds and the beauty beyond the canyon.

"Where do you go when you vanish like that?" I asked out loud to the fish. I thought to myself how odd it would sound if someone heard me ask this question to a trout I could not see.

It was a question of faith. The fish was still *there* somewhere in the current but I was no longer attached to it by my line. The connection had come and gone. Denial took its place.

Flooded with frustration and anger, I sat down on the sand and laid back. *What just happened? I ask for a sign and now this?* I thought. "I'm trying to read more into this. It was just a snag the whole time!" I said out loud, laughing and crying at the same time.

I asked a more direct question. "God," I said. "Why is it that I can feel so connected to you and then suddenly I hit a snag and it's as though you don't exist?"

Lying there next to my belly boat, staring out past the canyon, I expected to feel utterly alone. As I laid there on the sand, tears streaming down my cheeks, I realized that the question had already been answered.

There is no knowing. There is only faith.

Perhaps losing that fish exactly the way I lost it was meant to be. Who was I to think it was supposed to happen any other way?

The light in the canyon shifted as I made camp by the side of the river. After dinner I made a small campfire and got out my journal to write a letter to my brother.

"There are so many unspoken words. You are on a journey that is essentially a solo effort, and yet the battle you wage is universal. Your struggle is completely separate and totally connected at the same time.

"The relationship between brothers is not unlike that of a man and woman in marriage; the marriage part may be superficial but if there is true love then the spiritual connection is almost palpable. And yet, as much as two people can be one, it is an impossibility.

"Our connectedness began when we started this journey in the same place, forming and developing in the same womb of our shared mother, and later in her home.

"My first memory of you is looking up at a smiling face—you! As my big brother you were always my protector, and now I know that even when you are gone from this earth, you will join our deceased brother Paul to look over me. I must never doubt our connection.

"All that I have to do is look up at the stars above tonight, here in this ancient canyon, to see the great mystery beyond the stars. It takes great wisdom to see beyond the stars, but today for a brief moment, I did."

I don't know *exactly* how to connect my experience in the canyons, and my connection to a Higher Power on a daily basis, but I do know that there must be spirits—perhaps angel anglers and explorers who have gone before us—who provide us guidance when we allow ourselves to let go of doubt. Perhaps in the canyon that day Everett Ruess' spirit, like an angel, was lying next to me, as I grieved over the impending loss of my brother. I heard a voice whisper through the canyon, saying, *"While I am alive, I intend to live."*

Today, if I am very still and connected, wading in the river running through my soul, I can sense the presence of my brothers. This is spirit. It speaks to us in love. It tells us that no betrayal or abandonment can ever harm us when we trust that the universe is on our side.

God, You are all-knowing and have planted secrets that lie just below the surface of the current that we might uncover and discover. Thank You for granting us the courage to catch and release our greatest fears.

Preserving Life's Metaphors[2]

"It is those we live with and love and should know who elude us."

—Norman Maclean,
A River Runs Through It

AS I'VE BECOME MORE EXPERIENCED ON THE RIVER, I'VE LEARNED HOW fragile the river ecosystem can be. Whether it's mining, timber cutting, cattle ranching, or construction, man can profoundly affect a fishery over time.

A good example is the Big Blackfoot where Norman Maclean and his brother fished in *A River Runs Through It*. By the early 1990s, the Blackfoot was hardly worth fishing because of serious environmental degradation that had gone unchecked for years.

While location scouting, we decided the river was useless for the film. Debris causing clear cuts, mine waste, and cattle grazing had severely reduced the scenic value, trout population, and water clarity. Luckily, the attention the river received from the movie helped bring it back and today the Big Blackfoot is one of the best examples of what people can do to help damaged and neglected cold-water fisheries.

This kind of turnaround cannot take place without the support of a new breed of fly fishers. As fishing pressure increases around the world, the onus of conservation increasingly falls upon this new generation to

---

2   Excerpted from *Shadowcasting: An Introduction to the Art of Flyfishing* (2000). Reprinted with permission from Clinetop Press.

stand up for the rivers they love. The river is a special place that can never be replaced, a finite resource that we all need to protect.

A River Runs Through It is more than a great fishing story; it's one of the greatest pieces of American West literature in the world! I often wonder what would have happened if Norman and Paul had grown up on the Blackfoot of the 1980s when its trout population was at a record low. Maybe the Macleans would have given up on fly fishing and their story never would have been told. How can you have a story like that without fishing on the Blackfoot as a central metaphor? You can't.

I thought about this notion as my father and I sat on the porch of my brother's small house near San Francisco.

"Hey, look at this," my dad said, pointing to a headline in the *Chronicle*. "Salmon Spawning up Devil's Gulch. First Time in Ten Years."

"Where is that?" I asked with enthusiasm.

Within minutes we were in the car and on the way to Devil's Gulch, a half-hour drive from the Golden Gate Bridge. What is left of salmon and steelhead runs in Bay Area streams have been protected for years, so this spontaneous expedition would be to sight fish, not catch them.

After spending the last several days of rain at my brother's bedside, it felt good to see the sun again. My dad, my brother, and I had fished together most of our lives. We would have asked my brother to come along to search for fish but this was one trip he could not take; my brother was dying of cancer.

We parked the car at the Devil's Gulch sign and walked up the small foot trail. The swollen creek below roared as it cascaded over the boulders, forming a series of pools and runs. We kept walking, our eyes peeled for spawning salmon. After an hour of searching, night began to fall. The river seemed barren of life.

"We should turn around," my dad suggested. "It'll be dark going back."

"One more run," I said as I hurried up the side of the creek. My dad followed me to a small waterfall.

"There," we said together. Sure enough, a twenty-inch coho salmon washed over the waterfall. In the pool below, it tried to swim upstream to keep steady but its fins were too weak. By all the black markings and white fungus, it was evident that this salmon had already swum up from the ocean ten miles away. The valiant fish had spawned and was now fighting a losing battle with Mother Nature.

We stood there in silence, surrounded by fern and dripping oaks, watching the salmon struggle in the fading light of the gulch. As hard as the fish kicked with his tail, the current gradually flushed him downstream until he disappeared around the bend.

Dad put his arm around me and for a moment we both stared into the eddy of the pool in front of us.

"The circle of life," my dad said softly.

As we walked down the trail, I thought about how these streams were once packed solid with red and silver bodies. Native American shamans used to have visions of these creatures swimming up the veins of the earth: Shamans who lived in magic villages under the sea who disguised themselves as fish to visit people of the river.

In the old days, the salmon died for a purpose: to give the river life. They fed their offspring and provided food for eagles, bears, and other animals. As we walked down the trail in silence, I began to see that life is a circle. That with every death there is a birth, and that maybe the approaching death of my brother, Kresser would not be an error or a sacrifice, but like the salmon, a poetic dance.

My brother died from cancer three days later. He saw his first child grow to be six months old. Three hours before his death, my sister gave birth to a baby girl in Oakland.

My father witnessed the birth of his grandchild and the death of his son in the same day. Just as the salmon die to give the rivers life, my brother died as part of a mystical song to the roundness of life.

Gratitude[3]

"We are always starting over. We are always beginning again. Something within us or about us changes: it is time to be moving on. Change is seldom easy. A friendship, a favorite spot, a familiar lifestyle slip away, and nothing is the same. The important thing is to be able to sacrifice at any moment what we are for what we could become. May God grace our turning points with patience and peace."

—Miriam Therese Winter

THE HOLIDAYS ARE ALWAYS THE TIME OF YEAR FOR ME TO REFLECT ON WHAT I have and to realize that we can take nothing for granted. One Christmas, after fishing and skiing, I had a stroke and came as close to death as I ever have.

I had never tried fishing at Christmas. In years past I'd been too into skiing and snowboarding in the winter to even give it a second thought. But that year, I decided to give myself a special present. I spent the morning with my parents, my sister's family, and my wife opening presents, then bundled up and took off.

My parents lived on the Roaring Fork River and upstream from their house there were only about three homes before the road ended and the river entered a three-mile section of catch-and-release-only water accessed by a small footpath. Ice and snow choked the river in the

---

3   Excerpted from *Shadowcasting: An Introduction to the Art of Flyfishing* (2000). Reprinted with permission from Clinetop Press.

Canyon Section. It was a gorgeous cold winter day, around 24 degrees in the shade, but quite warm in the sun.

I found a slow-moving section—a place that I knew was deep and typically held many fish nearby during the summer months. I took off my gloves, opened my fly box, and selected two distinct patterns that caught my eye—size twenty midge larvae. Just as my fingers began to numb, I finished the clinch knots and slipped my cold hands back into my gloves. After my fingers warmed up some, I pinched on a small weight four inches above the first fly and an indicator about six feet beyond that. To catch trout in the middle of winter in the Rocky Mountains you typically have to use midges. In this case, I decided to fish them deep since there were no bugs flying and no fish rising.

For the first half hour or so I thought that this gift to myself was a bit foolish; ice caked around my line, forming a solid heavy film that made the line feel like a string of lead. I had to clear the ice off every other time I cast; if I waited too long, the ice would get so thick that it could not pass through the eye at the tip of the rod. I had to take my gloves off and use the heat of my fingers to melt off the frosty coating. Standing alone on the ice shelf, convincing myself that it would bear my weight, I went through the arduous process of casting and clearing repeatedly until I developed an efficient routine.

On the third cast I hooked a nice rainbow that gave a surprising amount of fight. Since trout go into semi-hibernation in the winter months, they typically don't fight much. This one did and it made me smile.

After catching three or four darkly mottled rainbows, I walked down the snow-laden path toward home and peered down onto a small eddy formed by the white ice floes.

To my surprise, a well-proportioned rainbow held there in the current and stood out against the pale background as obvious as a beacon in the night sky.

It moved slowly, sipping midges on the surface. I hastily bit off my line at the weight, tore off the indicator, and tied on a piece of tippet and a dry fly. To avoid approaching the fish from in front of its line of sight I took pains to find a section of cliff where I could "ski" down the slope in my wading boots. I snuck up behind the fish—crawling on my gloves and wader-knees. The eddy current was tricky and I made several drifts to no avail.

On the sixth cast, I watched the fish swim slowly over to my fly and suck it in. I lifted the rod tip and hooked the fish.

Like its brethren, it put up a surprising fight. Just before landing it, the leader strafed over a ragged piece of ice and snapped the fish off. I shrugged my shoulders, reeled up the line, and headed home to get warm. The very fact that I had sight-fished to a nice rainbow on Christmas Day and hooked him on a dry fly was a wonderful gift.

The next day, my wife Mollie and I went skiing at Snowmass, which seemed saner than fishing, especially with temperatures plunging to the zero mark. We were skiing down our last run when a strange feeling came over me. We stopped midway up the mountain when the left side of my face began to tremble uncontrollably, my eyesight blurred, and I felt like I was going to pass out. I yelled out, "Mollie, something is happening to me!" It was one of the most frightening experiences of my life. After about fifteen seconds, I yelled to her. "Make it stop!" She grabbed my face and shook my head vigorously.

"You're gonna be fine," she said matter-of-factly, and I snapped out of it.

Mollie thought I'd had a seizure. When I explained the situation to nearby ski patrolmen, they took the situation far more seriously than I expected.

I had a more pronounced partial seizure in the sled on the way down and another two-minute episode in the clinic. At one point I had so much adrenaline coursing through my body that I forced my way up and off the gurney even though seven attendants tried to restrain me. I thought I was dying from a stroke or a heart attack! The truth was that no one knew why I was suddenly having seizures—least of all me, whom the medical personnel shortly knocked out with Valium.

I was rushed to Aspen Valley Hospital in an ambulance with Mollie by my side. My parents met us at the hospital, where a CAT scan and MRI revealed a bleeding mass in the upper part of my left brain. "It is highly unlikely that this is cancer, or even a benign tumor," the doctor informed us. "We think it is probably what we call a cavernous hemangioma." After many more tests and scans there—and at UCLA when I returned home—the condition was confirmed.

The doctors told us that I probably had this "vascular malformation" in my brain since childhood. This type of condition doesn't manifest until it "reveals" itself through a seizure or severe headache when you're in your twenties or thirties. Although it is well-documented, it is relatively uncommon. While the condition was curable, I was told that without an operation the next episode could be fatal. I later discovered that Olympic gold medalist and track star Florence Griffith Joyner died in her sleep during such an episode—from a ruptured cavernous hemangioma. Even though the decision to operate was technically "optional," at my age I had no choice but to go for it.

After an angiogram and similar opinions from three top vascular brain surgeons, I underwent a four-and-a-half-hour surgery on January 13, 1998 at UCLA. There was never any real risk of being left with "neurological deficiencies," and the doctors had given me a 98 percent chance of success before the operation. That did little to alleviate the nagging thought that I might never wake up or recover. When I came to in the recovery room, vomiting liquid, I was relieved to hear them say that the surgery went even better than expected.

I only spent one day in intensive care and another three days in the hospital. It took close to three months to fully recover, and although there have been no lasting effects from the surgery, I was an invalid at first. I could barely walk around the outside of my house the first day, and only with the assistance of my wife.

After the first week, I graduated to walking around the block, then slowly worked my way up to a mile, then two miles. I slowly regained my health, and what could have been a cancerous brain tumor or a paralyzing stroke turned out to be a wake-up call that has allowed me to appreciate my life more than ever.

In April, I returned to my parents' house by the river that I love so much. The Fork looked a lot different now with the snow and ice of December long since melted, and there were a few more fishermen. I quietly found a place upstream and around the corner from the nearest angler, where I could be alone, and I began casting for the first time since December.

It was a gorgeous spring day, around sixty degrees in the shade, but quite warm in the sun. I found a section that was moving slowly—a place that I knew was deep and typically held many fish during the summer months. Instead of midges, I tied on two utility nymphs: a Prince and a Hare's Ear. It was nice to be in that routine again. Tying the clinch knots came more easily than I expected. A tear of joy fell from my face and smoothed the last knot before I pulled it tight.

God had released me back to the waters where I belonged.

Sting of the Butt Monkey

"Your competition is not other people but the time you kill, the ill will you create, the knowledge you neglect to learn, the connections you fail to build, the health you sacrifice along the path, your inability to generate ideas, the people around you who don't support and love your efforts, and whatever god you curse for your bad luck."

—James Altucher

AT MY SECRET FISHING SPOT, MY GOOD FRIEND CLARK RECENTLY SCHOOLED me like never before. Hiking for hours among the yucca, chaparral, and scattered pines, I felt the familiar tightness of anticipation that only a trout junkie knows. My remedy, as always, was to simply slow down, look around at the wide expanses, and remind myself that this was not about results. I had been sworn to secrecy about this fishing spot by my friend Bernard, who shared it with me a few years ago. Clark is the only other soul that I have taken into this mythic place that feels more like Montana than Los Angeles! I knew there were some rainbows in this system over twenty inches. Fish greed began seething in my veins and I had to breathe and tell myself to *be here now. You will get to the river soon enough.*

Within thirty seconds of arrival by the banks, I didn't have the patience to first set up my rod. I impetuously ran down to the water and scanned the small creek. Out of the corner of my eye, I saw what looked like an otter swimming along the side of the creek below me. *Otters don't live here.* Suddenly, the object revealed itself.

"Clark, quick," I yelled. "There's a huge rainbow, nearly two feet long, moving up the river and he's eating dries!" Clark peered over the bushes.

"I see him!" he replied.

"Keep watching him to see where he goes," I demanded.

Hands shaking slightly, and with a reminder to "*breathe*," I quickly set up my rod and tied on a size 14 Stimulator. Witnessing this large trout cruising and sipping insects on the surface was akin to a cocaine addict seeing white powder on the mirror. I tested my knots then moved stealthily towards Clark, who was now a hundred feet upstream.

"He's still feeding pretty good," Clark informed me as he pointed to the repeated dimples on the stream.

"This is like being in New Zealand all over again." I had just returned from the South Island, fishing for trout considerably larger than the one in front of me.

I positioned myself low and behind the fish. While I had been setting up my rod, Clark had observed this fish moving aggressively up in the shallows, then sliding back down, sipping an assortment of insects in routine fashion. Having just returned from the Queen's Chain, I knew a big happy fish when I saw one.

Using a couple of false casts away from the trajectory, I pivoted and cast with my new three-weight seven-foot rod. The fly landed short of the still feeding fish. I was used to fishing a much bigger nine-foot-six weight. I heard a snicker from the bushes in the vicinity of where Clark knelt.

"Cast it up higher," Clark whispered, as if I didn't recognize the imperfections of my first cast!

"At least I didn't line him," I replied loudly without whispering back.

"Don't fuck it up this time!"

I worked another six feet of line into my cast and laid it gingerly four feet in front of the beast. As the fly was about to land perfectly, a gust of wind blew it short and to the side of the fish. The fish immediately slid over diagonally, looked up, then ever so slowly lifted its lumbering head and opened its mouth. The feeding motion was so *slow* that it triggered a "delay" response in my cerebral cortex as "God Save the Queen" played in my head. After what seemed like an eternity of self-restraint, I lifted my rod tip the way my Kiwi guides had taught me.

There was just one problem. I was in Southern California, not New Zealand. New Zealand guides are famous for telling their clients to wait at least two seconds before setting the hook; the trout there are so large that it takes more time for them to open and close their mouths!

Instead of feeling the bend in my rod and hearing the explosion of a jumping trophy rainbow, the line went slack. The spooked fish bolted upstream and disappeared.

"*You suck!*"

I thought the words were coming from the same inner-voice sabo-teur that had shouted "God Save the Queen" before Clark appeared from behind the bushes. "*You suck!*" he shouted again. "It's like you for-got to set the hook. What happened?"

I just stood there, trying to regain my composure.

Clark waded closer. "In case you didn't hear me, You sucked!"

"No, you said, '*You suck,*'" I replied.

"That beauty slurped up your fly but you were late on the hookset!"

"It's a new rod and it's short!" I said, getting defensive. "I brought the wrong reel since your truck ran over the one I lent you."

"Oh, so you're blaming *me* for your defeat?!"

"Hey, at least it wasn't on camera," I said.

Clark unloaded. "I bet you have a bunch of those on the cutting room floor. So what, you want a consolation-prize trophy like the ones they give all the kids in Little League now? You've been coddled too long by your TV crews, making fishing shows where they can edit out your mistakes! Dude, admit it, you sucked!"

"Very funny, Clark," I responded.

"I just wanted to see that fish up close with a dry fly in its mouth," Clark said.

"Me too."

"But alas," he said, and turned to me with a devious grin. "Now it's my turn!"

Clark and I have been good friends for more than twenty years, having originally met while serving on the board of the Southern California chapter of Trout Unlimited together. He is an accomplished angler but we had only started to fish together a few years before. As good friends sometimes do on the water, we like to compete. We also like to give each other a good dose of shit!

In a sport like fly fishing, competition on the water is considered *dégoûtante,* French for beastly or obnoxious. As one of the most traditional, genteel, and literary sports on the planet, fly fishing requires the tempering of the male ego so that more sublime elements of the sport might surface. However, on days like today, my ego was not about to be sublimated. Being a "famous fly fisherman," this failure in front of my friend hurt like a punch to the stomach. My only path to redemption was *repartee* and retribution.

As the host of *Adventure Guides: Fishing Edition* on the Outdoor Channel, I developed a reputation for guides and guest anglers giving me grief when I missed fish, but I had never been subjected to the kind of abuse that only a true fishing buddy could dish out.

"You see, Dietsch, after all these years hanging around 'yes' people on your TV shows who don't want to tell the 'King' that he's naked, I'm sticking a mirror in your face to show you how this doughy white boy looks like without fishing attire. And now I am going to point to the fat tire around his waist!"

That's when I noticed that Clark's mouth wasn't moving. Was what I heard my own inner voice? Perhaps the kind of negativity that may have inspired the missed fish in the first place? I started to wonder if Clark had said *any* of the things I had just heard.

Fly fishing is amazing in that it focuses you on one solitary objective and somehow shrinks the world down to size. My wife sometimes complains about the time and money I spend on the sport but the truth is that fly fishing on a quiet stream is a lot less expensive than therapy!

Any time I make a mistake on the water, I check my mind to make sure it is not due to self-sabotage. However, in this instance, Clark had my goat. He knew I was in my head! He mimicked that familiar *negative self-talk* and was now going for the jugular.

While I can fish streamers, I am not a streamer-fisherman like Clark. I prefer to nymph-fish when forced to use sub-surface techniques. Using the former technique, the angler strips a minnow-like fly, whereas the latter imitates an insect that is dead-drifted below the surface with the current. As a lifelong streamer-fisherman from Michigan, Clark has studied the art form and spent long hours tying patterns, reading books, and watching DVDs on the subject matter.

We had worked our way upstream about a hundred and fifty feet and now stood at the edge of the first relatively deep pool.

"I am now going to catch your fish with a Green Butt Monkey," Clark announced confidently. He pointed to the two-inch-long double-hooked contraption that looked like an articulated eel-like creature at the end of his line.

"You're what?" I asked, my heart sinking. My initial thought was that there was no way Clark could catch a spooked fish on a streamer, and part of me wanted to push him into the eddy swirl for even trying! I had never seen someone go after a fish that had been spooked like that, not even with a guide, nor had I had someone talk to me in such a condescending tone!

Clark explained that "our" fish had likely sought sheltered water—a deep pool where it would feel safe. "A fish that has been spooked like this won't likely take a dry fly or nymph, but their brains tell them to eat. I'm placing my bet on the fact that he fled under there." He pointed with his fly rod to the undercut bank like Babe Ruth pointing to the bleachers.

Clark then laid a cast up into the lower corner, just below the overhang in the riverbank, a likely spot for the trout to hide. He stripped the streamer fast through the emerald waters but no one followed. Lifting up for a back cast, he adeptly cast farther upstream, just above a prominent rock that defined the hole. On the third strip, the fish finally flashed.

"There she is," Clark said. "She turned."

The fish turned away. If I had any doubts about a spooked fish going after a streamer, it vanished with that display.

"I don't believe this," I replied in astonishment. A bead of sweat rolled down my forehead.

"She wants to eat again," he said. "Just like a bass, stripping something this big and delectable elicits a predatory response you won't get with an insect pattern."

Just then, as if responding to my fear, Clark's line went taut, and my trepidation erupted from the depths.

"I hooked your fish, Dietsch!"

"You're a freakin' fish burglar!" I yelled out weakly. The fish didn't fight too hard, probably because it had taken its first initial run without a fly in its mouth some ten minutes earlier. After a couple of twists and turns and a few attempted jumps, *my* fish turned on its side and Clark brought it swiftly to the bank. He scooped the fish into his wet hands and smiled as he displayed *my* Scarlet rainbow.

"That's a gorgeous fish, Clark. I would congratulate you but there appears to be a piece of meat hanging out of the side of its mouth disgracing what should have been a small delicate dry fly."

"Yes," Clark replied, "and that *dry fly* is conspicuously missing, isn't it?"

"If I'd known that you were a piscatorial kleptomaniac I would never have invited you to my secret spot!"

"Don't worry, John, I won't tell anyone this story. It will stay exclusively between you and me." The most devastating part of that comment was that he was serious.

"That hurts! Now I have to write about it so you can't hold it over me the rest of my life! Bastard!" My face flushed red with the understanding of just how much had been lost to wounded pride. "Even masters fuck it up."

"Say *whatever* you need to say to soothe your bruised ego friend 'cause you'll never live this one down," Clark replied with glee, while resuscitating the beautiful rainbow.

"I admit that is the nicest fish I have seen in these parts in twenty years. But I am not feeling even one iota of fish envy," I lied.

"Yip, could have been yours...on a dry fly...but you failed, and when that happens I have to step in and clean up your mess."

"How about you kiss my Butt...Monkey?!"

"Oh, a little sensitive about the sting of the Butt Monkey?" he replied, applying his hemostats to the barbless green streamer in the fish's mouth. "I don't blame you."

The word "sting" hung in the air.

"You realize what you have done, right, Clark?" I asked as he let the large, four-pound fish swim away. "You just declared war."

"You can have the waterfall pool," Clark offered in a patronizing tone. It just so happened that the waterfall pool was one of the biggest ones on the river.

"I'll take your charity. Anything to get that Butt Monkey off my back." We began to wade downstream together then split up so I could fish the waterfall pool. I tied on a Green Butt Monkey.

I cast through the pool to no avail. I did get a short-take at the top of the riffle—a piece of intelligence that I stored away for the ensuing battle.

Normally, my friends and I fish apart for hours at a time, walking upstream fishing nymphs and dries, without seeing each other at all. But today, with what was at stake, I was not about to let Clark get far out of my sight. Once he disappeared around the corner, I followed him downstream and vowed not to let him out of my sight for the rest of the morning. I wanted revenge.

Over the next two hours neither Clark nor I saw another fish, let alone caught one or got a short take. I couldn't live with myself if Clark caught another big one using a streamer. I was completely off my game!

Each time I came to a pool I would scan it for fish, throw a few casts with the Butt Monkey, see if I moved any fish, then move quickly on to Clark's water. When Clark would see me nearby, he'd get this perturbed look on his face and say, "Dietsch, what are you doing here again? I mean there is *no way* that you're fishing *your* water thoroughly. And now you're standing right where I was about to cast."

I ignored Clark's protests and instead told him that I fished this very same section last time there was a big runoff, right where I was standing, and I hooked ten fish on a nymph. I told him that because of the geography of this terrain, the fish are very migratory, and because of water temperature and other factors that I could not figure out, they simply were not in this section of river right now. My friend Bernard Yin, who originally told me about this spot, once told me that he and a couple of local biologists believed that some of the native, resident rainbows in Southern California are remnant steelhead. They have this theory that in certain fisheries rainbows mimic steelhead behavior and in the spring become highly migratory, particularly when the fishery is above a reservoir, lake, or other sizable piece of water. In California, due to drought and extreme temperature fluctuations, rainbows tend to move around a lot, sometimes surviving in small stretches of water fed by underground springs. When the creek is about to get too low, they return to the lake.

Clark and I turned around and started fishing some of the pools we had skipped or fished through too quickly.

"What are you doing, running?" I asked Clark, who was moving fast on the other side of the willows. His gait had gone from a fast walk to a jog.

"I am just trying to get to my hole before you do because I don't trust you anymore."

"What are you talking about?" I asked, breathing harder than usual.

"You keep blowing off *your* water to fish *mine*, and I keep giving you the best water, but you still want mine. What is up with you?"

"I thought we'd fish together today," I replied.

"Is this how you always fish?" Clark asked.

"Do you always steal other people's fish?" I questioned back with a grin.

We both laughed.

The best pool of the day waited ahead of us like the prettiest girl at closing time. Testosterone wafted up from the water.

"Let's fish this hole together," I offered.

"Together?" Clark asked with a laugh. "Like couples yoga?"

"Take turns," I said. "You know, like hopscotch."

"Do I have a choice?" Clark answered.

"Not really. My water. My rules. And I'm still smarting."

"Get used to it," Clark said as he began casting.

"Funny."

I stood and watched Clark fish the pool. Clearly, his idea of hop-scotch was different than mine.

In the narrow throat of the river, I waded up behind him. He cast awkwardly and shot me a menacing look. When his forward cast land-ed, he waited a beat as it sank and then stripped his streamer through the pool with authority, picked it up, and tried again. On the fourth go-round, I heard him swear. He was snagged in the tree behind us. I smiled broadly as I waded up next to him, rod in hand.

"Ah…. Bummer. Looks like your Monkey's in the tree and you're going to have to leave this pool open."

"No way, Dietsch," Clark rebutted. "I'm not done yet."

If I took a cast now I would be pushing our friendship. Instead, I walked back and fished Clark's streamer out of the tree without poach-ing his hole. I told myself I deserved a medal for not throwing a cast with my rod.

"The only reason my fly is in this tree," Clark's voice strained as I reached up high with both hands to pull down the willow branch, "is because you were wading directly behind me where I needed to back cast."

"I just wanted to see if you planned to hook me in the head," I joked. Clark knew I had nowhere else to wade if I wanted to get parallel to him. He was agitated by this experiment of fishing in such close quarters and that by this time last year I had caught a dozen fish on a nymph and Clark had landed half a dozen on a streamer. Today we'd only caught one between *us*!

The thought that I might get skunked drove my decisions. I knew that I needed to take a break—have lunch, meditate, or take a nap—but that was the farthest thing from my mind. I was experiencing my familiar obsession that occurs on the water—and I would not stop fishing until I was catching!

Clark cleared his line and waded back up. On the next cast, he exclaimed that three different fish had chased his streamer. From my vantage point I could not see well enough into the pool but I believed him. After many more casts with no luck, Clark turned to me and finally said he was done. It had been nearly four hours since Clark landed the big rainbow and I was still fishless!

I accepted the invitation to fish *his* pool but decided to rig my rod with nymphs and an indicator. I tied on a twenty-incher Stonefly pattern with a size 14 Copper John dropper. I used a split shot just three inches above the lead fly that was tied to a nine-foot leader. As Clark sat back to watch me and eat his lunch, I cast into the oxygenated pool's deepest part. Seconds into the first drift, the indicator dipped and I set the hook. A sizable rainbow bent the rod, then catapulted out of the water in a frothy explosion. Because this pool was so deep and full of bubbles, the fish fought and jumped with vigor, giving my three-weight a hefty bend. He made four distinct runs and refused to come in. Eventually, the feisty trout acquiesced and I carefully beached him on shore.

The fish only measured fourteen-and-a-half inches but had beautiful markings and broad shoulders. While some of the fish in the system were stocked, this fish appeared to be wild. After releasing this healthy specimen, I proceeded to hook and land two smaller fish right in a row. Clark watched from across the river without any bravado or false compliments. It felt good to get the skunk off my hands and to catch fish in a pool where he had first dibs! Getting a few of *his* fish under my belt was like paying small payments on a debt. I was just getting started!

"See," Clark said, "I told you there were three fish in that pool!"

Not being a nymph fisherman, Clark's interest was piqued by my success. Having taught and written about nymphing for years, I was as comfortable using this method as Clark was comfortable throwing a weighted streamer. I had to wonder what the lower section would have been like if we had fished those deeper pools with nymphs.

I offered Clark my rig to nymph-fish while I ate lunch. I am amazed how many accomplished dry fly or streamer fishermen are either intimidated about nymphing or know very little about it. The truth is that nymphing can often catch fish when no other technique can—and it requires tremendous skill to be good at it.

The concept of nymphing is not much different than dry fly fishing. In most situations, the angler wants to cast his fly three-quarters upstream, up and across, using either weighted nymphs or flies and a split shot or other small weights if needed. While some anglers use a section of colored line as an indicator, I prefer to use indicators that mark my line and have little or no buoyancy. Still others use floats, yarn, or small balloons—all indicator methods that I have experimented with. The concept, of course, is to imitate an aquatic insect or other relatively stationary piece of food (that is, a worm, shrimp, or egg) in a way that the fly sinks quickly and can be "dead-drifted" with the current to a feeding fish. Of course, the most sporting and productive form of nymphing is done with no indicator and is often referred to as European Nymphing. Typically, fish will feed on nymphs, underwater, for as much as 80 percent of their diet. Nymphing is a staple of my arsenal and I really wanted Clark to give the technique a test drive.

Watching Clark nymph-fish, I noticed that he was drifting his nymphs through the slower, smoother water in the midsection of the pool. All the fish I caught were in the most highly oxygenated part of the pool at the top of the run, where the water was still white and just starting to slow down. Fish tend to be where high-water temperature is an issue. I remembered the short-take I had gotten earlier in the day. It had taken place in the same exact piece of oxygenated riffle water that Clark had yet to fish.

A dastardly thought entered my mind.

"Clark, would you mind if I showed you a demo cast?" I asked. "Your drift has too much slack in it."

"Be my guest."

"You're doing fine." I said, smiling politely. "You're just not casting in the right place."

He hesitated as he handed the rod back to me. I shuffled into the current, positioned my feet, and cast greedily into the perfect riffle water.

"Your line needs to be a little tauter," I said as I took line in emphatically with my left hand, "and you should extend your arm out a little farther, up high—shoulder level like this—to get a good…." I paused for effect as I jerked the rod back.

"*Hookset!*" I yelled out as if to say, You Suck! I immediately felt weight in the line. A large rainbow flashed beneath the riffle and took line deep into the pool.

"That's a good fish, Dietsch," Clark said.

"This just feels so right…when it is *so* wrong!"

While I played *his* fish, praying to God that the line would not break, the valiant salmonid made repeated tug-of-war twists and turns in the deep grey-green pool, occasionally thrashing the surface.

There is something about having an eighteen-inch rainbow on your line that just makes the whole world feel better. Perhaps it's related to some deep-seated insecurity about my manhood, but my day went from zero to hero with one really dirty cast.

"You stole my first fish of the day so now we're even," I stated, slowly bringing the fish in and clutching it in my hands with avarice. I held it up for a few photographs and smiled. The silvery-black rainbow with shades of red and mottled spots felt heavy in my wetted hands. I felt like Clark and I were finally even.

"It's maybe seventeen to eighteen inches, Dietsch," Clark offered. "Nice fish. Mine was nineteen to twenty inches and it was a lot fatter."

This war may never end, I thought.

"Score is four fish to one. Or should I say four stolen fish to one stolen fish!" I said, laughing.

The nice fish slipped through my hands and disappeared back into its ephemeral lair. Clark came over and I wanted to tell him about the compulsion I had that had practically ruined my marriage, derailed my business, and otherwise wreaked havoc in my life—all in the pursuit of one-upmanship. But alas, I sighed relief and let the river soothe that part of my soul. At that moment, I realized that no fish large enough existed to fill that particular void.

"Sorry," I said. "I didn't mean to catch your fish!"

"Yeah you did," Clark laughed and I joined in.

I handed him the rod and went back to eating my lunch.

I offered to guide him using nymphs "with no more demos," but the suggestion was rebuffed. I was sincere in my offer but Clark may have figured that accepting was a form of surrender. While he never said it to my face, he did not want me stealing any more of his fish. He suggested that we separate and fish alone along entirely different sections of water. He was trying to get rid of me, but who could blame him at this point? He had had enough of my *revenge fishing,* but I wasn't finished with him yet! I convinced him that we should at least play hopscotch, trading sections of a hundred yards or so at a time.

We moved upstream above where he had caught that first troublesome trout of the day. As I walked through the water, I spooked a fish, then another and another. Some were nice size. The midday air was warm now and this section of water was full of pockets and runs. I began thinking that the small waterfall just above where I caught Clark's fish would be difficult for fish to swim through except at high water. Using stimulators and other attractor patterns like Royal Wulffs and

H&L Variants—as well as small grasshopper patterns—the dry fly fishing suddenly turned on. Whereas the stretches below were devoid of fish, these upper reaches held quite a few large trout.

I was about to pass Clark and move upstream to fish a new section when he said that he had just spooked an eighteen-inch rainbow.

"Dietsch, watch this!" Clark boasted. I turned to watch him lay a perfect cast with his grasshopper in a narrow slot about three feet wide. As soon as the fly landed there was a large gulping sound and a *big* fish leaped out of the water. It quickly turned and the mini-monster charged upstream and disappeared in the reeds.

"Broke him off," Clark gasped.

A few seconds of pause made my next comment all the more satisfactory.

"*You suck!*" We both cracked up.

"Bad tippet," he replied.

"Likely story," I answered and gave him a fresh spool of 4x. "You can keep it. It's your consolation prize!"

"So you think you're the winner now?" Clark asked.

"There is no winning. Only love!"

"Love of big fish!" Clark replied.

"That too!"

In my book the score was now even, if only in the category of *repartee* and trash talk. As for catching the biggest fish of the day, that award is rightfully on Clark's shelf, not that it really matters in the end.

In the river, my goal is to have a spiritual experience that is not connected to competition or results: to seek something far more healing and connected than whether my fish or your fish is bigger.

Sometimes, when big fish are at stake, it feels like the gloves come off and bare my ego's need for validation. When I compare myself to others who have more than I do, I create an expectation that ends in resentment. When I gloat because I have a bigger fish than anyone else, it says more about my own inner self-doubt than anything else. When I am in that competitive cycle, where I am more body than soul, it is nearly impossible for the river to remind me of my shortcomings. I can only reflect to see how I was blinded by shame.

As the late Lefty Kreh—one of the most well-known and beloved fly fishermen of all time—once told me, it is better to be of service and to help people rather than to compete with them. In the end, we are all released back to where we came from, and no one will ever take the biggest fish home.

> *Infinite Divine Being, why do I sometimes block Your presence because of my need to get my way? In the end, we throw everything back to You anyway, so why do I often let my pursuit of fish, money, or pride become more important than my spiritual path? What relationships have been affected by this selfish propensity and my fear of being less than someone else? Help me find balance in my life that I might be at once present to Your will.*

Snow Blind

"The ultimate lesson all of us have to learn is unconditional love, which includes not only others, but ourselves as well."

—Elisabeth Kübler-Ross

I LOVE MY SON. HE MEANS THE WORLD TO ME. WHEN JOHNNY WAS BORN, I stood in awe by my wife's side as I witnessed his little head passing through the cavity of her body and into the world. His eyes were wide open and stared right into mine. As our eyes locked, in an instant gaze I burst into tears. As I described the experience later, I told my own father that I had a distinct feeling, at that exact moment when my son and I first met each other, that Johnny would be my teacher.

When Johnny was fourteen, our family took a ski trip to Snowmass, Colorado. I remember standing at the top of the mountain and scanning from peaks above to the valley below. For a brief moment I visualized the snow beneath my skis as sustenance for the river, a frozen reservoir whose contents melt into the veins of the earth when the light of the sun defeats the shadow of winter.

Prior to the trip, Johnny made me promise that I would not make him ski any double black diamonds. The last time we had hit the slopes, I unknowingly took him down a double black diamond run in the late afternoon, where the shade of the mountain had frozen the face into a solid sheet of ice! Johnny spent the majority of the descent in terror as he side-slipped down inch by inch, frozen with fear.

On this last day, I did convince my family to ski three black diamonds and they all skied the recently groomed runs with ease. I had been a ski instructor for more than a decade many moons before and was filled with pride as I watched my wife, daughter, and son *ski the blacks*. I took photographs of my family standing beneath the black diamond signs: "Promenade," "Slot," and "Zugspitze," which I later hung near the kitchen for my friends to see.

As we rode to the top after lunch, I pointed out the double black diamond run that sat at 12,500 feet. We could barely make out two black dots descending in zigzag formations down a steep face, kicking up rooster tails of white powder that disappeared into the ominous cornice just above the run.

"I can ski that, Dad," Johnny said.

"Are you sure?" I secretly hoped that he would not back down.

"Do you think I can? It doesn't look that steep."

"Yeah, it's not *that* steep," I said with some trepidation.

"Is it *a lot* steeper than the black diamond that we just skied?" he asked.

"Yeah, but that steep section at the top is short, "I told him. "You can do it."

"OK," Johnny said in agreement. "Let's do it!"

"OK," I repeated. "Let's do it!"

"You sure I can do it, Dad?" Johnny asked again with hesitation.

"Look, Johnny, you don't *have* to do this," I said. "It is not a good idea for us to go up there if you are not fully committed," I said straight-faced, offering a way out.

The long pause was awkward.

"OK, Dad, I want to ski off the top," he replied

"How can I be the man if you're the man?" I yelled with enthusiasm. I had wanted this for my son since he was a young boy. "You're on!" I shouted and skied toward the lift with him following cautiously behind.

The temperature gauge that had read fifty degrees just an hour before now read thirty-nine. The wind had kicked up. Although the forecast was for a 40 percent chance of thunderstorms, the weather predictions over the last two days had called for similar storms and none had materialized. Looking out to Snowmass Peak, I noticed that it was now cloaked in a cloud of snow, yet this obvious sign eluded me. *A decision has been made.*

As we schussed to the mountain's highest lift, the snow racing beneath my skis began to harden like my resolve. *My son does not want to let me down.* I didn't realize I was projecting onto him my own inequities: the expectations, the judgments, the people-pleasing that had grown out of the relationship with my own father and which had become the parental voice inside my head.

We were skiing the Cirque. There was no going back.

In John Bradshaw's book, *Healing the Shame that Binds You,* he identifies shame as the motivator behind our toxic behaviors: "the compulsion, codependency, addiction, and drive to super-achieve that can break down the family and destroy personal lives."

Shame is a powerful force that is often passed down from generation to generation. Shame differs from guilt. When we feel guilt, it is a negative feeling about something we did. When we feel shame, it is a generalized feeling of negativity about our self.

As humans, we avoid shame at all costs. We employ other emotions to cover up shame or act out in ways that are hurtful to ourselves and others, sometimes creating emotional scars that are difficult to heal.

Anger and rage often serve to hide feelings of shame, especially when one's self-esteem is threatened. I would like to pretend that I am so self-aware that I can avoid acting out of shame, but for me shame is often too deceptive to identify until it is too late.

According to Bradshaw, when people try to super-achieve, it can sometimes be a mask for shame. Shame can destroy marriages, jobs, relationships, and lives. In families, it is often passed on like a cursed family heirloom unless it is identified, discussed in the open, and laid to rest instead of brushed under the rug.

Johnny and I skied up to the Poma lift. Johnny had only taken a surface lift like this once before, so as he slid past the lift attendant and placed the disc between his legs, the spring-loaded pole jerked him off his skis and he fell.

"No! Not like that!" I yelled at the top of my lungs, scared that he was about to get injured. "Let it go!"

At the last second, Johnny let go of the disc between his legs and it shot off uphill, swinging aimlessly from the cable and smashing against the first tower with a *bang*.

"That was a close one," the attendant said to Johnny as he climbed back to his feet and, getting a quick lesson from the attendant, tried again, this time with success.

While riding the lift behind him, I remembered the first time I felt I had disappointed my parents on the snow. I was attending a boarding school called Holderness in New Hampshire. I went there in part because the retired coach from the U.S. ski team worked there. I had a goal of making the U.S. Olympic team, even though I had started ski racing nearly a decade later than many of my peers. I always wanted my father to come watch me ski race, but he never did. Instead, my mom flew all the way across the country from California to watch me. Halfway down the course, right as I raced by where she stood, I took a spectacular fall. *She traveled all the way across the United States only to watch me crash and burn.* I was crushed. Later, she assured me that I would do better next time. A year later, when I told my father I was afraid of failure, I remember him remaining silent and not knowing how to respond.

His silence spoke volumes. *It is a disgrace to fail.*

I made the University of Colorado ski team my freshman year. We won the national championship, but I never made the A team. I did win several races but nothing on a national level. I even made some money ski racing and teaching professionally part-time, but in my mind I never achieved the goal I had set.

Approaching an elevation of 12,000 feet on the Poma lift, Johnny and I reached tree-line with another five hundred feet of vertical until the top.

The sky turned dark and the wind began to howl. It started to snow sideways. Johnny was underdressed in a T-shirt and my old blue Patagonia parka. I watched him ahead of me on the Poma lift. For a moment, I saw myself climbing to the top.

As the storm enveloped us, I became *Snow Blind* to any difference between the two of us. *Snow Blindness,* or photokeratitis, is a type of temporary eye damage caused by snow reflecting UV light, but today the "snow" blinding me was a form of self-centered fear that I projected unconsciously.

At the top, John Frederick Dietsch Jr. detached from the platter lift and skied to a stop. I got off and skied to him.

"You sure we should do this?" John Jr. asked me, our jackets flapping loudly in the wind.

"You cold?" I asked in response.

"Just my ears," he replied.

"I told you to wear something warmer," I said in an annoyed voice, as I flipped the hood of his parka up and over his helmet then began to adjust the draw strings to form the hood around his face and goggles.

"I'm fine," he said with a pause.

"It is getting pretty icy," he complained.

Then he asked again, "You sure we should do this, Dad?"

"We did not come up here to turn around," I responded flatly, perhaps repeating something I had heard from my own father, and my father from *his* dad.

I felt irritated that John Jr. would even consider a retreat. The notion seemed "soft," and being from Southern California I was really sensitive to John Jr. being a *city boy* who was not comfortable in the mountains. Blind to the deteriorating weather, I could no longer recognize his face through the goggles and small opening in the borrowed jacket.

"It won't be icy once we drop into the Cirque," I replied as I skied past him. "The snow will be nice."

As I skied across the flat portion of the glade, the wind began to howl and large flakes began blowing horizontally. I glanced back, half expecting that John Jr. would not be in tow. The snow beneath my skis crunched as we trudged toward the abyss. This desolate stretch of tundra extended across a flat snowfield full of obstacles that took us down to the entrance of the gate at the top of the Cirque. The visibility decreased by the second and I grew impatient. *We need to pass through the gate and drop into the bowl to get out of the wind and avoid lightning.*

At some point on the long traverse, I crossed an invisible line. A blur of reality and fear convinced me there was only one way down: To climb back up would mean hypothermia or death by electrocution, and to descend further along the ridge meant getting lost or having to ski something even steeper. The question of how I managed to bring my son into this treacherous predicament increased my self-doubt and made my resolve all the more intractable. *There was only one way down!*

When we arrived at the entrance to the top of the run, I could barely make out the way the slope dropped off precipitously just beyond the ropes that separated us from the gated entrance.

Johnny stood behind me, his posture indicating fear and hesitation.

"Dad, I don't want to do this," Johnny cried, his voice trembling.

"You're crying?" I asked the question more like a statement. I recognized my own fear and, in a moment of compassion, side-stepped up to him and gave him a short hug.

"I know you are scared," I said, "but there is only one way down."

"I'm not doing this," John Jr. replied, his fear turning to anger. "No fucking way, Dad!"

The light had become so flat that there was no way to tell up from down without a tree or a rock to give a skier any reference. No wonder Johnny was scared half-to-death! This fact somehow eluded me. In my mind, this was all or nothing!

"Fine," I yelled sarcastically as I abruptly kicked off both my skis.

"We will walk all the way back up to the top of the lift and get hypothermia or hit by lightning. Is that what you want?" I asked.

"Why'd you take us here, Dad? The run is closed anyway!" He pointed to the rope that crossed in front of the gate.

"No, it's still open," I said, pointing to the gate that appeared to be open at the far end near a red sign.

"Well, I'm not going," he said again.

"Yes, you are, because we have no alternative," I insisted. "You can do it, John," I added, as much for myself as for him.

"You're insane. Dad, you said this would be fun and sunny and soft and that I could ski this." His voice cracked. "Why did you do this to us? You are such an asshole!"

"Don't talk to me like that," I responded firmly. "We have to get down the mountain."

"No, Dad," he replied, "*you* have to get us out of here. It's not my fault."

"OK, I'm sorry that I put you in this situation but I did not *see* this snow squall coming, and there is only one way down." I put my skis back on and headed to the gate. I expected Johnny to be behind me, but instead I saw him walking away from me in his ski boots. He had left his skis behind!

"What do you think you're doing?" I asked.

"Getting out of here," he answered. "That's what."

I looked at the gate below me and did a double take. A rope stretched across the entire opening. The run was closed.

I unlatched the rope and slid through to the other side.

"Come on, John," I said. "Go back and get your skis. This is the only way down." Then I added, "If we stay up here this could become a lightning storm and we don't want to be the tallest object."

Johnny had completely tuned me out. Rather than walking back up the mountain the way we had come down, he was now horizontal across the top of the Cirque, parallel to the ropes that warned skiers of the giant cliff-bands below.

Standing at the top of the closed run, a red rope between us, I was about to shout, "Where the hell do you think you're going?" but I stopped.

I recognized that my son had found a simple solution I had not considered. In the panic-like atmosphere that the storm in my mind had created, I only saw one way out; climbing back up was not an option. But suddenly with his guidance, I recognized that if I followed him along the top of the Cirque for only a few minutes that we would reach the relatively flat area around the midsection of the Poma lift where we could ski down easily.

I gave in, shut up, and followed my son. I looked down at the oblivion below the ropes, where there was virtually no difference between the snowy sky and ski slope below. The idea of skiing the Cirque suddenly became ludicrous.

Retreating from the closed run, I side-stepped up and underneath the rope, past the gate, and grabbed Johnny's skis. He wasn't turning around. In fact, he was now leading the way out. When he finally turned around and saw me carrying his skis, he offered to carry them himself and to let me lead, but I simply shook my head, knowing that part of my penance was to follow him, shut up, and carry his skis.

As we walked in silence, the snowfall was so intense that the blizzard-like conditions caused Johnny to disappear from my view even though he was only just a few feet in front of me. Johnny knew we were safe as long as we stayed on the open side of the rope.

As I skated across the top of the Cirque, I had this pervasive feeling that I did not measure up to other dads, and that I'd done something wrong. I was ashamed.

Later, I started doing some work around my sense of shame, where it comes from, and how I might better identify it before it blindly hurts me or someone I love.

The decision to ski off the top of the mountain with Johnny had come from reasonable beliefs and values—ones a lot of dads have: *My son is a good enough skier to ski off the top of the mountain,* or *When you decide to do something, you do it.* But all black and white judgments that don't allow for individual variation or exceptional circumstances have the potential to shame. They require perfection and create an impossible standard. These beliefs demand perfection and a lack of individuality. They say that if we fail, just one time, then we are failures. These beliefs dictate that if we opt out of doing something we say we're going to do, we're not good enough.

There are other ways that shame distorts our thinking besides causing us to buy into all-or-nothing values. Shame makes us *imagine* that we know what others think about us, often basing this on inconclusive evidence or projections. On the mountain that day, shame subconsciously told me that to turn back meant that people would think the Dietsches are quitters.

Shame often causes catastrophic thinking: *We're going to get hit by lightning standing here so we better ski down a closed run with no visibility!* The imagination is a powerful force. Under the influence of shame, it can be crippling.

In hindsight, the pain and paranoia of shame clouded my ability to see the world as it really was. Bradshaw says that when under the influence of toxic shame, you meet someone new and are sure he or she thinks you're inept because you believe, *I'm not good enough.* When your wife is tired and distant after a long day, you imagine, *She doesn't love me anymore—because I'm not lovable.* When you believe each chest pain might mean your heart is failing, your thought might be, *Of course my heart will fail because nothing good ever happens to me. Life won't let me be happy.* Shame "self-perpetuates negative occurrences," according to Bradshaw.

When my son and I hiked to the far side of the Cirque, the clouds parted just as fast as they had descended. Winter folded back into spring with blue skies and freshly coated peaks glistening as far as the eye could see. I put Johnny's skis in the snow and he stepped into them without saying a word.

As I stood next to the middle of the Poma, looking at the beauty that began to unfold around me, I embraced my son.

"What's wrong, Dad?" Johnny asked.

"I'm sorry, Johnny. I'm sorry about what happened up there. I thought I was trying to protect you. I never meant to harm you."

"It's OK, Dad," Johnny said. "I know you really wanted me to go down your way, but I found a better way out."

"I know."

"I hope you're not disappointed," he said.

"No, far from it. I am really proud of you! When you were born you looked into my eyes, I couldn't explain it, but I knew you were special. Today, you were my teacher."

Later, when I finished telling this story to my dad, he was confused and said, "Fathers are supposed to teach their sons—not the other way around."

"So my story didn't teach you anything?" I asked him in response.

"Well, now that you put it that way," he said with a chuckle, then he looked at me in earnest. "Today, *you* were my teacher."

For a moment, I was that boy standing on the edge of a precipice afraid to disappoint my own father; I too revolted and took my own path down the mountain. Having the courage to look at our own dark shadows directs us toward the light that causes them.

God, grant us the courage to face up to our own shame so that we might see the light, break the chains, and in so doing refrain from perpetuating the toxic cycle.
I pray that I may let my child live his own life
and not the one I wish I had lived.
Therefore, guard me against burdening him
with doing what I failed to do.
Help me to see his missteps today in perspective
against the long road he must go.
And grant me the grace of patience with his slow pace.
Give me the wisdom of knowing when to smile
at the small mischiefs of his age.

And when to give him the haven of firmness against
the impulses which he fears he cannot master.
Help me to hear the anguish in his heart
through the din of angry words or across the gulf of brooding
silence.
And having heard, give me the grace
to bridge the gap between us with understanding warmth.
I pray that I may raise my voice more in joy at what he is,
than vexation of what he has done,
so that each day he may grow in sureness of himself.
Help me to hold him with warmth that will give him friendliness
to others.
Then give me the fortitude to free him to go strongly on his way.

A PARENT'S PRAYER,
Anonymous Author

CHAPTER 5

Faith from Fishing

Old Man's Knot[4]

"...All good things—trout as well as eternal salvation—come by grace and grace comes by art and art does not come easy."

—Norman Maclean

WANTED: MEN IN THEIR SEVENTIES, MUST BE
excellent fly casters, meet at Sacajawea Park,
Sunday, 10 a.m. Bring fly fishing equipment.

This was how the advertisement read that I had placed in the local Livingston newspaper in the summer of 1991. I figure it was the first casting *casting* call in the history of film and television....

On Sunday morning about thirty Montana locals showed up—weathered faces, ribbed hands, wool shirts, hats from the attic, and fly lines cutting through the air. Robert Redford, the director of the film *A River Runs Through It,* was looking for the "Old Man" character who appears briefly at the beginning and end of the film. He was to play Norman Maclean in his seventies. One by one, I had the men sign in and walk toward the end of the dock by the pond in Sacajawea Park, near the Yellowstone River. Within just a few short seconds, I could tell whether the gentleman was a good caster or not.

Surprisingly, only six of the men had decent casts, and really only two of them had the "right look"—the older man was in his late

---

4   Excerpted from *Shadowcasting: An Introduction to the Art of Flyfishing* (2000). Reprinted with permission from Clinetop Press.

seventies, and had deeply etched wrinkles, cool blue eyes, and thick tufts of white hair. However, he somehow looked too fragile to me. The younger man, in his early seventies, seemed to personify the Norman Maclean I had heard about—strong, opinionated, handsome, and direct. Having chosen these two men among the thirty, I dismissed everyone else and began casting with them, talking to them, and tying knots. The latter task would be asked of the character on camera in the film's final scene, so it was important to see how each of them carried it out.

The younger gentleman showed me how he tied his flies to his tippet with a clinch knot. He slid the tip of the monofilament into the eye of the hook with finesse, and smoothly wrapped the tag end around the line, just above the hook like a spiral. Then he adeptly brought the tag end through the opening in the line, just above the eye. He wet the line with his mouth and pulled tight. The whole process took under thirty seconds.

"There," the younger man said with a smile, "a clinch knot."

"Impressive," I replied.

The older man stood to my left, and although I was half expecting him to be watching the younger man—his competition—tie the clinch knot, I realized that he was concentrating on tying his own knot. I excused myself from the younger man and walked over to the older gentleman.

"What are you tying?" I asked him.

He looked at me, with a sheepish grin, and simply said, "My eyes aren't so good anymore."

His hands shook with the ferocity that only old age could induce. Between his poor eyesight and his trembling fingers, he had yet to simply thread the tippet through the eye of the hook, let alone tie the knot.

"Do you know how to tie a clinch knot?" I asked patiently. Again, the painful smile crept up on his mouth, and he shook his head slightly.

"No," he replied, pausing for a long moment.

A red light went off in my head: *This guy can't even thread the line through the eye of the hook and he doesn't know what a clinch knot is.* Suddenly, I thought that the older man could never work as Norman on camera, but I kept the decision to myself.

"I tie a turle knot," he continued. "Do you know what a turle knot is?" he asked.

"I've heard of it," I replied, "but I don't know how to tie one." *Perhaps you could show me how to tie it if you could just thread the damn line through the eye of the fly!*

He continued to tie his turle knot, twisting the line so that it formed a loop that would slide back against the eye of the hook. I felt the clock ticking in my head, and imagined a camera rolling thousands of dollars' worth of film while this man's trembling hands attempted to tie this ancient knot.

"You know this is an old knot," he said to me, his hands shaking like the San Andreas fault. "Most everybody used this knot in the old days here in Montana…. It takes a bit more time to tie than a clinch knot, but I think it's a better knot—worth the extra time."

I felt like saying: *Do you really know what time is worth here?* I could hardly contain the voices in my head—an impatience had developed in me from being around a film crew twenty-four hours a day. Impatient, and thinking there was no way we'd hire him for the role, I didn't allow the old man to complete his turle knot. As a result, I have never really learned to tie a dependable turle knot. However, I did learn something very valuable about myself that day.

That afternoon, I presented Redford with the photographs of both men and explained that each of them had a beautiful cast. I then gave him my opinion that I felt the younger man might be a better choice since the older man would probably have a terrible time tying a knot on camera.

"Why's that?" the director asked astutely.

"Because his hands shake violently. He can hardly even thread the line through a fly!" I replied with exasperation.

Redford paused for a moment and looked at the picture of the older man again.

"Excellent," he answered. "I'd like to meet the older man tomorrow."

His name was Arnold Richardson, and he had moved to Montana from Maine in his retirement where he worked as a fly fishing guide. To play the part of Norman Maclean was an honor and the memory for a lifetime. The shaking hands struggling to tie a knot at the end of the film are a trademark of the movie and tell a story in themselves. Looking back at it, in my haste to "succeed," I lost my sense of compassion, and in so doing I missed the magic that unfolded right in front of my eyes. I missed the message on the backs of the old man's veined, transparent, and leathered hands—the yearning that any man his age, feeling the passage of time, might have for younger days—but most of all the gentle acceptance that indeed those days were gone forever.

Today, I too am approaching my years as a senior whether I want to accept that reality or not. I think of "the words under the rocks" that Norman wrote of, and while I may not have recognized their meaning when I was younger, I believe we can all develop the ability to understand what the river is trying to tell to us. I believe this was Norman's message and now his words are among those under the rocks, along with the words of Arnold, who passed away on December 6, 2010 at the age of ninety-six.

I believe these words ask us to surrender to the source of the river, wherever we believe that source to be.

As Norman wrote, referring to the words from our loved ones that can be found in a river bed: "Some of them are theirs."

The Science Behind Water's Spiritual Qualities

"Our tradition is that of the first man who sneaked away to the creek when the tribe did not really need fish."

—Roderick Haig-Brown

WATER IS THE MOST SPIRITUAL COMPOUND ON EARTH. COMPRISING MORE than 60 percent of the human body and over 70 percent of the earth, water has always been sacred to aboriginal cultures and virtually all religions worldwide. Today, modern man has lost his reverence for water. He is more concerned with how to harness or use it than he is with maintaining its integrity. Water is bottled, dammed, polluted, overheated, and rerouted at an ever-alarming pace. We take it for granted. However, its importance is unrivaled in nature. Increasingly, scientists perceive water as a conscious organism that is self-creating and self-organizing.

In the bestselling book *The Hidden Messages in Water*, and in the film *What the Bleep Do We Know!?*, Dr. Masaru Emoto captures water's expressions: he developed a technique using a powerful microscope in a freezing cold room, combined with high-speed photography, to capture the images of newly formed crystals in frozen water samples. Just before freezing each glass of water, Emoto would expose each water sample to a different emotion, image, or sound. He discovered that the crystals revealed similar changes when specific, concentrated thoughts were directed at them. For instance, he found that water from clear springs and water that has been exposed to loving words showed intricate, brilliant, and colorful snowflake patterns. On the other hand, polluted water and water exposed to negative thoughts formed incomplete, asymmetrical, and dull patterns. Even negative labels such as bad or ugly produced frozen crystals not nearly as intricate or aesthetically pleasing as water vessels with labels like good and beautiful.

Considering our bodies are made up of mostly water, Emoto's experiments seem to prove how thoughts and emotions can affect the body's water content. From the perspective of a fly fisherman, it is little wonder that a creek filled with spring water has such a delightful and calming effect on the human body. Emoto's findings also show how our thoughts, emotions, and attitudes may deeply impact one another and the environment around us. Emoto's insights pair in many ways with Norman Maclean's quote about the ability of rivers to carry certain messages from our ancestors: "Under the (river's) rocks are the words and some of them are theirs...."

Quantum biology postulates that water binds all of life into one vast network of energy, allowing instant communication and coherence. Because water is essentially a closed system on earth, the same water molecules have cycled throughout earth's history since the beginning of time: rain, rivers, oceans, evaporation, and back again. Water cycles over and over throughout the world in a profound circle that is the very fabric of life. Many believe that this infinite cycle and its fundamental properties for life gives water a unique *spiritual memory*. The water molecules that are inside you now have likely been a part of other living beings in the past.

In a world increasingly beset by water-borne disasters, changing our relationship with water on a personal and cultural level can help bring our world back into balance. Water is the ultimate regulator of our body's physical and spiritual health in much the same way that it regulates the health of the earth. When our body is not in balance, the natural water cycle within us is threatened, just as the earth's natural water cycle causes things like drought, super-storms, and mega-hurricanes when the planet's equilibrium is out of balance.

When we are around running water such as rivers, waterfalls, or ocean waves, many of us perceive a feeling of well-being; we are in sync with nature. Running water, in particular, emits negative ions; falling or splashing water causes splitting of neutral particles of air, freeing electrons that attach to other air molecules, causing a negative charge. This charge has been proven to alter brain waves, enhance mood, and stimulate the senses. Metaphysicians are just beginning to understand how the unique properties of water, including its unusual density, affect energy states in life forms (that is, water is denser as a liquid than as a solid; ice floats on top of water).

Just ask any number of recovering cancer or PTSD survivors who have joined retreats through organizations like Project Healing Waters, Reel Recover, or Casting for Recovery. Many will tell you that fly fishing on rivers was a catalyst for their miraculous recoveries. I have been a buddy/guide on a couple of Reel Recovery retreats where I sat in a circle with men battling cancer, then took them out onto rivers armed with a fly rod to help battle their disease with the help of the healing qualities of trout waters. While I am no scientist, I have witnessed how these men respond to the mesmerizing cadence of a river. For me, being a part of these retreats has made it crystal clear that water has healing powers that we are just beginning to understand.

For the warrior fly fisherman who is innately connected to the rhythm and flow of the river, the notion that these waters contain wisdom lies at the core of our pursuit. Having reverence for waters replenishes the soul and gives us bearing. There is an unspoken bond between those of us who *know* we arose from waters: when our time comes, water is where we will return.

We no longer fish for food; at the highest level of our pursuit, we fish—sometimes unknowingly—to connect ourselves with a power greater than ourselves.

Great Spirit, You live in the waters all around us, all-powerful and in us. Grant us Your wisdom to be at peace with all that was, is, and will be. Let us be connected to one another through the grace of Your never-ending flow that we experience every time we step into Your waters, reborn again and again in Your love and grace, knowing that in each molecule—and within us—exists the entire universe.

The Nature of Impermanence

"Whenever someone dies, a part of the universe dies too. Everything a person felt, experienced, and saw dies with them, like tears in the rain."

—Paulo Coelho

"WHAT THE...?" I ASKED OUT LOUD, LOOKING OUT AT THE ONCE VERDANT, now desolate Bear Canyon in the San Gabriel mountains of Southern California.

I expected that the resilient trout here would have survived higher up in the creek, but as I walked on the trail overlooking the canyon, I realized that something cataclysmic must have happened.

Gigantic piles of debris, twenty feet high, lay in deliberate piles surrounded by sand and gravel that stretched from one side of the canyon to the next. What had been lush undergrowth, small trees, and a series of boulders was now scoured beyond recognition. This was no longer the lovely place that I had remembered and cherished for decades. It now looked like a giant desert-like arroyo. Massive logs, the size of Volkswagens, lay in the middle of Bear Canyon, evidently having been placed there by a monstrous current.

This doesn't make any sense. We are in the middle of one of the biggest droughts in California history and I am looking at the aftermath of a gargantuan flood.

There is no way that this damage is from runoff; there was never enough snow for that this year. But there have been no big winter rains either. So when did this happen? How did this happen?

Disoriented, I retraced my steps from earlier that day. The morning had started at Northview High School in West Covina, some twenty miles away and four thousand feet down the mountain. I helped my sixteen-year-old son Johnny carry some of his baseball gear so he wouldn't be late. It was 9:14 and the coaches wanted the boys to be on the field by 9:15! There in the distance stood Mount Baldy, one of Southern California's highest peaks. Also known as Mount San Antonio, the ten-thousand-foot mountain loomed in the sky like an old friend beckoning me home. Normally, the peak would have been enshrouded in several feet of snow this time of year, but for the last four years the local mountains had experienced a severe drought, and the peak was snowless on the southern and western exposures that faced the baseball field.

This peak has enthralled me like no other mountain on the planet. In the same day, I have skied two feet of fresh powder and then driven ninety minutes away to surf five-foot ocean waves—a feat that can only be accomplished in a handful of locales on the earth. I've also skied off its backside with Pete Olsen, the general manager of the ski area.

Pete was as much a part of this mountain as anyone I have ever known. He helped me produce TV commercials with extreme skier Scot Schmidt in the mid-1990s, where they both helicopter-skied off the top of the ten-thousand-foot peak. Twenty years ago, one of Pete's employees first told me about Bear Creek Canyon, where I planned to go fishing that day.

Looking up at Mount Baldy in the distance, I marveled at its wildness. While I loved these local mountains, I also had the utmost respect for them. Because of their proximity to the Los Angeles metropolitan area, the San Gabriels contain a power that is underrated. They are one of the steepest and fastest growing mountain ranges in the world, and something about that can elicit an ominous feeling in and around them.

Every year, hikers, skiers, motorists, and tourists are taken unawares by avalanches, fires, mudslides, flash floods, and all sorts of other bizarre events. While any mountain doles out punishment, there is a strange fabrication that sometimes accompanies a mountain so close to a megalopolis: people erroneously believe that an urban mountain like this is more forgiving than other mountains. *It's not!*

The San Gabriel mountain range is one of the youngest ranges in the world. As an Outward Bound instructor named Kaki once related to me, the San Gabriel mountains have the energy of a toddler: capricious, devious, naughty, and without any care as to how their actions might affect others. These mountains get their way and as much as we try to stop certain events from happening, the awesome power of nature helps to remind us about our place in the universe, and the impermanence of all things.

"Dad, come on. I'm gonna be late," Johnny shouted, breaking me out of my reverie.

"I'm heading up to Mount Baldy to go fishing," I told him. I shook his hand, wished him luck, and walked away. Because he was on the disabled list due to a shoulder injury, he wouldn't be playing. I set him up with a ride home and I left for Mount Baldy after the fourth inning, when the pitcher walked four batters in a row.

Within a half hour by car, I drove past a sign that read "Elevation 3,000 feet" about two miles before Mount Baldy village. Rather than continue on to Bear Creek Canyon, which had been my go-to secret spot for nearly half my life, I found myself getting out in a hurry, grabbing my fly rod, and scampering down the hill to the main artery of San Antonio Creek. If people had been watching, I would have reminded them of a Labrador Retriever seeking a ball in water! I had to get to the creek and cast! I remember thinking as I walked fast down the hill, *This is not my plan. What am I doing?*

I hadn't even changed out of my Crocs or put on my fly fishing vest. I just grabbed my rod and headed to the creek as fast as I could!

Arriving at the bank along the small creek, I realized that *it had been the longest period of time in living memory that I have ever been away from a trout stream: six months!* I immediately recognized the low flow of the creek—a far cry from the robust runoff we often had in a normal snow year.

While I had fished the area during other drought years, this was one of the longest strings of back-to-back drought years on record. It hardly snowed in the San Gabriel mountains for forty-eight months in a row, so I had not returned to ski or fish for nearly as long. I was determined to test the waters to see how the trout had fared.

I decided to fish a tributary off the main stem of San Antonio Creek and to my surprise, I ended up catching a bunch of rainbows, some as large as ten inches, good size natives considering the drought conditions. Amazingly, the trout had survived the drought.

After fishing the main stem, I drove to the base of Bear Canyon, past several houses, and across the dry creek bed. I had never seen it this dry this time of year. I began hiking along the trail and looked out across the first big crossing. I stopped dead. The creek that had always been rock-strewn and full of small trees and plants looked scoured and barren, flat and smooth like a miniature flood plain.

In past drought years, I simply needed to walk up farther to find the fish. If there was no water down low, there was always water higher. That was one of the things that had kept this fishery so isolated; no one expected there to be fish anywhere because most of the time the tributary was completely cut off from the main stem. Uneducated anglers figured there was no water in the creek, but I could always find water and fish higher up.

I looked out at what used to be small boulders and there was only sand. The entire riverbed was gone. In the places where the larger trees still stood, the bark of the trunks about ten feet up had peeled off and flapped eerily in the wind.

"This is weird," I said out loud. "Looks like a huge flood came down here."

Suddenly, I heard a booming voice laughing from above. "No fish left in here." I looked across the canyon. A burly looking man stood on the balcony of a cabin. I had momentarily forgotten about the cabins that had been built into the side of the cliff above the creek.

"What happened here?" I asked.

"Back in August, it rained four inches in a single hour during a thunderstorm," he answered.

"It scoured the entire riverbed. There's nothing left!" My irritation and disappointment started to sink in.

"The wall of water was over twelve feet high," he said. "Destroyed all the footbridges and killed an Oriental."

"Excuse me?" I replied.

"An Asian guy was crossing down below where you drove up and his car got swept away. The windshield broke and he died. That bridge down there is brand new." He pointed to the footbridge at the base of the cliff that connected his home to the trail I was on.

"I used to fish right below that bridge," I said, pointing to the area of dry gravel and the trickling ditch that cut through it. "There used to be some nice fish in here."

"Well, they're not here anymore," he said. "They were all washed away in the flood."

I wish he had said he was sorry, or perhaps I should have said something, but there was this awkward moment where I felt small. I studied the area above the footbridge where my children had climbed giant boulders years ago, but they were gone. I figured that the boulders must have been six to seven feet tall. They had literally been swept away. I found myself far from the elation I felt earlier in the tributary to the east. My stream was no longer here; it only existed in memory.

I looked up at the burly man.

"Well, it's a nice day for a hike," I said. "Thank you for the info."

I walked back up the trail, secretly harboring possibility. *Maybe one of the big pools up the canyon had somehow been spared.* I had been coming here for nearly twenty years, and I imagined I would be able to find trout in this canyon for the rest of my life.

I first discovered Bear Canyon in 1995 when I descended the trail from the top of Mount Baldy after finishing a grueling run to the top of the peak. I was training for the Top of the Mountain foot race held every September. Near the village, I discovered this tiny trout stream. I didn't have a fly rod at the time but I remember spooking trout in one of the pools. I later found out that this canyon was the same creek that Pete Olsen's employee Nick had told me about.

After passing the craftsman house on the cliff, I would have normally descended into the streambed at the footbridge, but the idea of walking inside this unrecognizable canyon was too depressing. I needed to take all this in at a distance.

As I climbed higher on the path, parallel to the creek bed and twenty feet above it, I noticed that water was running down the center of the desolation, but there were no pools whatsoever. The stream was a small channel of water descending through a desert-like floor of smooth gravel. To the left and right, there were giant piles of rubble, some with large tree trunks or scraps of metal roofing protruding from them like grotesque forts.

What used to be a string of tightly knit trout pools had become a wasteland. While I had not named each pool, I had come to know each one intimately. I had memorized where the trout liked to hide, and I had fished there so many times that I could pretty much predict when a fish would take my fly or not. Often I would sight fish, trying to bypass smaller lies for ones that would hold "bigger" trout. Each time I had come here, it was like visiting an old friend. Today, it felt like my friend had died. *This was no longer a trout stream.* Nature apparently had other plans.

I turned a corner and came upon my pristine waterfall where I had previously come to meditate and renew, where I had taken numerous pictures of my children with a background of greenery and serene pools. It looked denuded and alien. The waterfall had been destroyed and there was barely a trickle flowing down the small bump that used to be a large drop. Conversely, I was glad to see that the giant Douglas Fir was still standing as though nothing had happened; several of these big trees had been uprooted and lay across the riverbed. This one had endured.

The creek bed became a mirror and the witnessing of impermanence unfolded in front of my eyes. I wasn't so much sad for the fish
or the inanimate rocks. I was sad for myself—and all sentient beings
who had to suffer, to live, and to die. At the same time, there was this
immense joy in the simple ability to see that everything changes; in that
moment I saw that nothing lasts, not even a trout stream with whom I
expected to grow old.

*No man steps into Bear Canyon twice, because the creek has changed and that
makes him mad!*

On some level, I was angry that nature could be so cruel, and I took
her actions personally.

The stillness calmed me, and in the soft winds I noticed a massive
tree I had never seen before. The flood had cleared away brush that
had obscured it before. The tree looked as though it climbed into the
sky forever, with no end to its crown. I marveled at its height and stature
next to the eviscerated streambed. As I descended the hillside, I saw that
it was actually two trees, side by side, sharing the same trunk. The one
on the right had a decidedly bigger circumference than its counterpart,
and as I stood there looking up at its magnificent growth, my hand
touched its skin. Next to the giant twin tree, a lone power pole provided
electricity to the cabins that dotted the canyon below. Someone had
wrapped a metal wire around the base of the biggest trunk to support
the pole. By the rusted appearance of the clasped wire, it was very old.

The biggest tree was the one connected to the power pole. A voice
inside me crisply explained that the biggest tree represented abundance
and the smaller one lack. They were born out of the same soil, but the
one most connected to humanity was abundance.

It was like the cord wrapped around the tree was connected to all
of humanity: the terminus for all that ever was or ever would be, right
there in Bear Canyon. I saw that we could never have abundance
without lack and that perhaps to experience one we must experience
the other.

I turned around and walked back down through the reconstructed streambed, accepting the fact that even the biggest pools of my old fishery were gone for now. As I negotiated past the new growth bursting from the stones, it dawned on me that something may have happened here that I missed. All those fish in the tributary on the opposite side of the canyon I'd fished earlier in the day were perhaps survivors of the flood: maybe some of the fish I caught earlier were indeed the fish that had washed down into San Antonio Creek and they had relocated in that tributary! I recognized that when the snow began to fall again and the drought was over, the creek would reform and the trout from San Antonio creek would swim back up into the canyon that I love. Who is to say that this could not happen in my lifetime? Regardless, all this would happen in God's time.

I approached the lone object I still recognized in the canyon before the flood. It was a massive tree trunk, the size of a minivan, still embedded in the ground, perhaps from a similar flood from five hundred years ago. I remembered its color, size, and location from a precious fishing trip I had taken to this same canyon when my children were six and eight years old. Back then, the entire length of the log on one side, three feet down and nearly fifteen feet across, was packed with thousands of crimson-colored ladybugs. I had never witnessed anything like it and my kids did not know if they should be excited or grossed out.

The memories of my children, at such innocent ages, can never been washed away by a five-hundred-year flood. However, nature reminds us of the importance of letting go of what was so that we can find acceptance for what is.

I began to wonder how much of what we see in this world is illusory. Even when I return to a place like the river, it may feel familiar and comforting, but is it really *the same?* I remembered a quote from Norman Maclean, "Something within fishermen tries to make fishing into a world perfect and apart." Perhaps the only perfection in life is our spirit beckoning us to be present to what is and what will always be; everything is changing all the time whether we choose to recognize it or not.

The next day, I researched the flood and learned that it took place on August 3, 2014: approximately eight months before my fishing trip that day. The National Weather Service determined that it was a five-hundred-year event, meaning that something like this only takes place twice in a millennium. Some 3.89 inches of rain fell in less than sixty minutes. I watched horrific news clips on YouTube and learned that the man who died in the flood was named Joo Hwan Lee, a forty-eight-year-old man from El Segundo, whose car got swept away in the deluge. I also came across something else. Pete Olsen, who I thought of before going up the mountain that day, died the night before the storm, on August 2, 2014. The very next day, his twin brother's home was destroyed by the debris field that forced his daughter Mindy to stand on top of her car as she watched the mountainside come crashing all around her in a rush of black ooze, boulders, and trees.

Like the conjoined wire wrapped around the twin tree in the canyon, I believe that Pete Olsen was connected with the energy of the flood that took place just after he died. Pete—who battled the mountain through floods, avalanches, and landslides when he ran the ski area—was now a part of the mountain. I like to think that the young mountain grieved when Pete Olsen passed away from pancreatic cancer early that same morning. In a temper tantrum that only a toddler can throw, Mount Baldy lashed out and its grief produced a tempest of unimaginable fury.

For thousands of years, aboriginals' creation stories have been born from these kinds of occurrences. In that canyon eight months after Pete's death, I sensed his spirit there among the alder, fir, and cottonwood. His is one of the souls that have been infused with the mountain's spirit, a part of God's world now, gently whispering as it trickles down the center of the new canyon, that we should be renewed not in our own way, but in His.

God, help me to release the past and its burden of wounded dreams. Help me to have clarity as if seeing a place or a person anew for the first time, even if what I wanted to see is not present anymore. Allow me to let go of the past so that I might make room for what is. Help me to detach from my grasping and to let go as if I were releasing something, like a magnificent trout, from captivity. And when I find myself questioning Your wisdom, allow me to be content with being in the question. Cultivate in me the knowledge that gradually, over time, the answers will come.... I welcome Your insight into impermanence, knowing that the only permanent directive is for me to discover Your will for my life. In Your time, Lord, in Your time. Amen!

The Confluence at Malibu Creek

"…. The Spirit too comes to the aid of our weakness; for we do not know how to pray as we ought."

—Romans 8:26

I BELIEVE THAT WATERS, PARTICULARLY WATERS ONCE FREQUENTED BY AN-cient runs of salmon and steelhead, have magical and spiritual qualities. I was baptized in water as a baby, and my indoctrination into spirit through Christ has always connected me in a mysterious way to water. There is ancestral energy in the waters of the earth that can heal us. These energies transcend the boundaries of church, temple, or syna-gogue. Healing waters are all part of God's kingdom. All waters con-tain the potential for what the famous mystic psychologist Abraham H. Maslow defines as *mystic or peak experiences.* According to Maslow, "The great lesson from the true mystics [is that] the sacred is in the ordinary, that it is to be found in one's daily life, in one's neighbors, friends, and family, in one's backyard." Clearly, Maslow forgot to mention *water*! For whatever reason, I have had these peak or mystical experiences in pris-tine settings around water, whether it is fresh, salt, or frozen. To ask my-self *why* I have encountered these kinds of experiences in and around water is like asking why I was born!

One time in New Zealand, I felt a presence while fly fishing under-neath a stunning waterfall. I distinctly recall the moment. I even wrote down the premonition in my journal. Two days later I discovered that my best friend's mother, Emily, had passed away right around the same time.

One of the strongest mystical experiences I have ever had took place more recently. I was invited to take part in a prayer circle in the Hawaiian tradition that calls for paddling out to sea on surfboards, forming a prayer circle, and spreading the ashes and flower pedals from leis. The circle was formed just south of the surf break called Malibu Point, made famous by the movie and TV series *Gidget*. Ironically, the creator of the *Gidget* series was the person whose life we were honoring. William Asher was one of the most prolific TV directors of his time, with a list of credits that included such hits as *Bewitched*, *Beach Blanket Bingo*, and *The Bad News Bears*.

The famous surf break is right at the river mouth of Malibu Creek, one of the world's southernmost steelhead fisheries in the Western Hemisphere.

I didn't know Bill very well, but being invited into this prayer circle of family and friends was an honor and a privilege. One by one, each person in the circle shared about their experience with this wonderfully creative man while sitting on our surfboards and holding hands. As each person shared, one thing stood out: as famous as Bill was, it was not this man's Hollywood achievements that he left behind, it was the love that he brought to this circle of family and friends.

As everyone talked, I began praying. I thought about how I had been scared to ask for Bill's help regarding my career. Suddenly, I had the distinct feeling that it was not too late! I made a silent prayer that I be guided.

After saying prayers and spreading Bill's ashes, along with flower petals, into the ocean, we all paddled in different directions, with many of us heading over to Malibu Point. Having surfed in dozens of locations across the globe, I had never surfed Malibu because it was so crowded all the time. Before I knew it, I was playing among its waves and catching some decent little peaks. I became totally immersed in this world of water and lost track of time. At some point the waves, the sky, the mountains, and the water all merged into one and I began to dip into some kind of altered reality. At first I was frightened and confused, and I cannot say for sure how long these dips into a dream-like state took place. The experience was like a series of déjà vu. It was like I was part of a dream, as though I had gone into a reverie or meditative state where I crossed into another dimension. It continued on and off for the rest of the day, with its peak taking place while I was surfing. It was like a spiritual or mental earthquake with several small "tremors" afterwards.

At one point while surfing, I remember panicking that I didn't know where I was or what day it was. When I finally paddled in I told my friend Charlie that I may have just had some kind of stroke! I was very frightened. The experience emulated my experience with the same people in the prayer circle, but we were doing the kinds of things you might do in a dream, a dream that I had apparently already had but was unaware of at the time. I was present, on my surfboard, but at the same time I drifted into what felt like another dimension, place, or past.

I was so disoriented that I just wanted to get back on dry land and find the "reality" that was "my real life." I had heard stories about epilepsy, Alzheimer's, and other brain disorders creating these types of experiences, so I was at first very concerned, especially because the lip of a wave had hit me smack in the forehead while paddling. Was this what had happened?

Once the panic subsided, Charlie suggested that I may have had a mystic experience. A peak or mystic experience, as described by Maslow in his book *Religion, Values, and Peak Experiences*, is:

> "…a visit to a personally defined heaven from which the person then returns to earth. This is like giving a naturalistic meaning to the concept of heaven."

This type of experience, like a déjà vu, is nearly impossible to describe. How can we experience a place without ever having been there?

Was it purely a coincidence that I was in a prayer circle just before having this experience?

It is debatable whether a déjà vu (which means "already seen" in French) is really a mystic or peak experience, as opposed to a "brain twitch." No one really knows why a mystic experience or string of déjà vu happens, or what it means. Increasingly, neuroscience believes that déjà vu is created in the temporal lobe of the brain. Epileptics, who have more déjà vu than ordinary humans due to their disorder, have been tested: the activity that causes the déjà vu can be isolated to this specific region. According to psychologist Akira O'Connor, from the University of St. Andrews, "One idea is that déjà vu is a sort of brain twitch. Just as we get muscle spasms or eye twitches, it could be that the bit of your brain which sends signals to do with familiarity and memory is firing out of turn."

As I researched, I came upon something called déjà rêvé, which means "already dreamed." Déjà rêvé is a phenomenon similar to déjà vu but instead of feeling like you have been here before, you feel like you have *dreamed* what is happening to you before, or what takes place in real life has already happened in a dream. When I first read about déjà rêvé, I felt chills go down my spine. There was even one account of a young man (with epilepsy) whose chronic déjà rêvé was so intense that he could hardly decipher between reality and his dreams on a day-to-day basis! This description was almost exactly what I felt in Malibu and two to three days after that (and have since experienced something similar, although less intense three other times, always around water). A recent study in the journal *Brain Stimulation* explains this chronic phenomenon that took place with certain epileptic patients who were able to recall a dream or have dream-like feelings (associated with a previous dream) while awake. It turns out that déjà rêvé, like déjà vu, can affect anyone regardless of whether they have had a brain injury or not.

When I first read about déjà rêvé and its association with patients who had neurological disorders, I was fearful that my history of brain trauma was to blame. I had brain surgery for a cavernous hemangioma in 1999 and more recently in 2018, I had what is called an episode of transient global amnesia (TGA). In the case of the latter, for six hours I was unable to form new memories. I said the same thing over and over again until finally, while about to undergo an MRI in the hospital, I started to remember who I was again. While it might seem that these neurological disorders are connected to my déjà rêvé phenomenon, I passed a number of brain scans and numerous neurological tests after the hemangioma and TGA events. According to my neurologists, it is impossible to link my déjà rêvé phenomenon to my past brain injuries which, they tell me, have completely healed.

I now believe that what happened to me at Malibu that day was perceived by my brain but not generated by it. From my point of view, my déjà rêvé is of a spiritual nature—not the onset of some terrible brain disorder! Sometimes putting too much emphasis on "figuring it out" etches God out. For me it is now clear that déjà vu, déjà rêvé, experiential phenomena, and mystic or peak experiences derive from spirit. In a world where the rational mind reigns supreme, we run the risk of forgetting that the place we come from and the place we are going to will always remain a *mystery.*

Déjà rêvé has offered me insight into the possibility that there are other dimensions. The concept of the multiverse and alternative realities are too complex to go into here, so suffice it to say that the feeling I get from a déjà rêvé is like receiving a telegraph transmitted with Morse code. Deciphering this code has helped me to recognize the message: *We Are Fundamentally Not of this Earth.* Perhaps we are not human beings having spiritual experiences at all. *We are spiritual beings having human experiences.* I believe that there is a numinous energy behind these kinds of experiences, and much like my other emotions, I am reminded to become more grounded in God's light and love; we are all children of God.

The Buddhists talk about duality; where there is something and nothing—heaven and earth—all occurring on the same plane at the same time. They recognize that we must be experiencing this duality in each moment whether we are aware of it or not. In many ways, this is a description of spirit; it is not entirely explainable, but it exists. This knowledge sets us free!

Deepak Chopra explains it in this way:

"The physical body is a vehicle for our consciousness. Consciousness is the basis of physicality, not a by-product of it. A radio receives and processes nonlocal radio waves and that allows us to hear the music or voice, but the radio did not make the music, nor are the radio waves dependent upon the physical radio for their existence. In the same way, our nonlocal consciousness is projected through our body and senses, but our consciousness is not dependent upon the body for its existence."

Using this same analogy, quantum physics has proven the potential for multiple dimensions. However, using the same analogy as Chopra, while there are many radio frequencies vibrating all around us, quantum physics asserts that we can only be tuned into one frequency, or dimension, at a time. Just like a radio, it is entirely possible that sometimes, for whatever reason, we hear two signals at the same time.

While mystical experiences like déjà rêvé and déjà vu have been recorded as activity in the temporal lobe of the brain, I am certain that mystical experiences do not originate inside the brain; these fleeting moments may be registered by the brain, but they occur as phenomena detected from source to guide us beyond everyday experience in the material. This is why shamans in aboriginal cultures often believe that people we often identify as mentally ill in Western cultures are actually closest to God.

There is an amazing freedom when we come to understand that a fish is not a fish, a wave is not a wave, and a river is not a river. While these *things* are all real, they are *unreal* too. This realization is the basic tenant of spirituality: life is actually one giant illusion, so relax, have fun, help others, and get out of the way. Spirit is always here, always present in us, but we have to be willing to tune in to its channel.

My prayer in the circle of surfboards was answered that day in Malibu; I had a glimpse into the eternal. Thanks, Bill! Thank you, Ashers! I am forever grateful to the spiritual qualities of ancestral waters!

Today I ask Spirit to provide me the willingness and courage to trust the unknown and therefore enter into the realm of infinite possibilities guided by our ancestors.

Angel with a Perfect Heart

"There is a River. Divine grace like a smoothly...flowing river yields refreshment and consolation to believers. This is the river of the water of life.... Happy are they who know from their own experience that there is such a river of God."

—Psalm 46:4

SPRING IS OFTEN A TIME OF PILGRIMAGE FOR ME. AFTER THE SNOWS OF winter relent their grip on mountain tundra, and the torrents of water, held back like so many tears, flood through the shadowed valley, I journey to that place, and I am healed. Recently I traveled back to the creek, called Cottonwood, where I first learned to fish for trout in the Sierras with my family.

It was here, just south of Mount Whitney, the tallest mountain in the continental United States, that I learned to put a salmon egg on a hook for the first time. Barely six years old, I marveled at the bubbling water-formed pools. I will never forget the moment I hooked my first trout: a field of electric current running down through the stream and up into my soul like a bolt of lightning.

I had come back here to remember someone I had forgotten. We had fished here long ago on numerous camping trips, and I had tried to impart my passion for fishing to him. Yet the memories of my brother Paul seemed to be trapped inside me somehow, like frozen waters reflecting their lament as mountain snows high above the ridge.

Instead of fishing this day, I decided to write in my journal.

Faith from Fishing

From as far back as I can remember, I knew that something was wrong with my younger brother Paul. He looked normal, except for the bluish color of his skin, especially his lips. When he was born the doctors told my parents that he had a number of heart defects, including Tetralogy of Fallot, a heart condition that causes oxygen-poor blood to flow through the body. In grammar school, when someone asked why Paul's lips turned blue when he exercised even a little bit, I replied that his heart was on the wrong side. Paul's heart condition made him very tired and irritable all the time because his body didn't get enough oxygen. Later I learned the medical term for one of his defects: dextrocardia. Literally the term means "right-hearted." Instead of having his heart on the left side like everyone else, Paul's heart was on his right. It would take me nearly five decades to recognize the perfection of having one's heart in the right place.

Paul was born on June 16, 1963. In order of age, it went Kresser, who was five years older than me; Gretchen, who was almost two years older than me; and then Paul, who was born twenty months later. He was about a year-and-a-half younger than me. When he was still an infant, he had an operation. The surgeons implanted a shunt into his heart so that his blood would get more oxygen. I learned later that the doctors took my parents aside and told them that Paul had little chance of living past the age of five.

Paul and I shared a room and a bunk bed in the house on the Westside of Los Angeles. Our father was a corporate lawyer, born and raised in East LA, who graduated from Berkeley and then Harvard law school at the top of his classes. My mom was the quintessential housewife. Growing up with a brother with a severe heart condition seemed very normal to me.

My siblings and I were instructed to always watch out for Paul; he was never to overexert himself, and he needed to rest if he walked more than a block or played for more than a minute or two. So we found things to do indoors like playing with blocks, listening to music, playing with model airplanes, drawing, and playing cards.

He wasn't allowed to run. If his lips turned a deep blue, which frequently happened, he had to rest. When it got really bad his whole face would turn blue and he would instinctively sit down on his haunches so the blood could flow more freely to his lungs. Paul could never participate in organized sports, but he could throw a baseball, or try to shoot a basketball, or even ride a bike at a slow pace. I often felt like it was my responsibility to monitor what he did and didn't do.

Since Paul couldn't participate in organized sports, he made up for it by becoming a big sports fan. We spent hours listening to the Dodgers and the Lakers on our red radio that was covered with sports decals. Jerry West, the famous Los Angeles Laker, lived up the street. One time, Paul and I went up to the West's house and saw a couple of kids playing hoops. Paul boldly walked down the driveway and introduced himself.

"Is Jerry West really your dad?" Paul asked to my chagrin.

"Yeah, he's our dad," one of the boys said as he looked away, bounced the ball at the free throw line and sank a basket.

I was surprised when Jerry West's sons asked us to join them.

When they saw that Paul couldn't reach the basket when trying to shoot the ball, they lowered the hoop with this cool machine we'd never seen before.

"You can lower the basket?" Paul asked with glee.

He made the first baskets of his life that afternoon and I can still remember the joy that achievement created: being able to do what everyone else did.

After a while, I could see that Paul was getting tired so I told him to squat down on his haunches. Seeing the blue in his lips and face, Jerry West's sons seemed alarmed. They asked what was wrong with him. So I told them he had his heart on the wrong side and that he didn't get enough oxygen because of it.

"He'll be fine," I said.

They looked at us strangely, and within minutes they took the ball and told us they had to go. That kind of thing happened a lot when

Paul and I were together. After that day, we went back to their house several times, but they always said they had to go and they went inside.

By the time I was ten, Paul had developed a whole set of his own friends, and although we had gone to the same school together (different from our other siblings) and had shared the same room our whole lives, we were becoming separate people.

On his eighth birthday, I remember feeling a little jealous about his popularity, wondering if people liked him because they felt sorry for him, or because he was different from everyone else. It never occurred to me that people loved Paul because he had such a passion for being in the moment, precisely because he innately knew how precious every day was.

One afternoon, when my cousins Tripp and Murray were visiting, the four of us rode our Schwinn Stingray bikes about a mile away to the Brentwood Mart to buy candy. In those days, parents allowed their children to ride bikes on the weekends as long as they were back home by dinnertime.

On our way back, when we were about a block away from home, my cousin Tripp and I decided to challenge one another to a race to the driveway!

"First one to the gate wins," Tripp yelled.

"Wait, Tripp," I said, knowing that Paul couldn't participate.

"Murray, do you mind staying back with Paul?" I asked quickly. "You'll need to go slow."

"On your marks, get set, go!" Tripp yelled as I turned to catch up.

I am older and I can't let him beat me, I thought as I pedaled like a madman, lifting off the banana seat and pumping my arms side to side as hard as I could on the ape-hanger handlebars.

With the driveway in sight I caught up to Tripp.

"I am going to beat you!" I yelled.

"No, you're not!" he yelled back. Neck and neck, we turned sharply into the entrance. I had angled myself on the inside and passed him on the right, through the gate and into the driveway, throwing my right hand into the air before clamping down on the right brake and skidding dramatically near the grass.

"I beat you," I exclaimed with pride, breathing hard.

"No, you didn't," Tripp yelled back as he skidded past me. "I beat you!"

"No, you didn't."

"Yes, I did."

Just then a horrific sound grew louder. We both stopped talking and heard this awful guttural heaving.

Looking back, it was the sound of spirit telling me that it's time. Through the next few minutes I left my body, and some say I never came back.

I remember things now in slow motion. Paul turning the corner and the color of his face. A tinge of purple I had never seen before.

His body didn't stop at all in the driveway and he kept going past us in slow motion, onto the grass, never pumping the brakes as though his bike had taken on a life of its own. It slid sideways and he collapsed, rolling to the side, his chest heaving in convulsions, and me running to him as fast as I could and realizing there was nothing to do except to find someone to save him, to save me. Frantic, I ran to the steps of my house.

"Mom, it's Paul," I struggled to pronounce through the distortion of fear. "I…think…he's…having…a…heart…attack!"

And my mom, now appearing in the doorway, her right leg in a full leg cast from a ski accident, running past me now, her hair bouncing as she screams, her crutches flying off to the side, running peg-legged to Paul, who lays on the ground, still struggling to breathe.

"What happened?" my mom shouts in panic. "What did you do?"

"We were racing and told him not to but he went anyway," I say.

"I told you not to race!" she shouts.

I start crying.

"It's OK, Paulie," she says. "You're going to be OK."

Suddenly, he begins to breathe better, shifting from the loud infrequent inhalations to more normal breaths.

"It's going to be alright," my mom says, hugging Paul and giving him a big kiss on the cheek

"It's gonna be alright."

Miraculously, Paul recovered. My parents didn't even take him to the hospital that day. As usual, we didn't really talk about what happened. We just went on like we always had.

One day, a few weeks later, my friend Larry and I decided to play a trick on Paul. He loved candy, and chocolate in particular.

So we came up with this idea. We carefully unwrapped a Hershey bar and ate the chocolate. Then we took a similar bar of ex-lax, all in a row like a chocolate bar, removed it from its packaging and rewrapped it, sliding it back into the Hershey bar packaging.

Another friend of ours had played the same trick on his younger brother and what we heard was that it made the other person poop and poop and poop, which at the time was a really funny thing you could do to your younger brother. We laughed hysterically as we stood behind the door and watched my brother eat the bar of ex-lax....

"So funny," I said.

"He'll shit like a horse," Larry said, trying not to laugh too loud.

That night, Paul became very ill. I had never seen him that sick before, all full of chills and fever and delirious underneath the blanket and my mom taking care of him.

The next day his condition didn't change. The thermometer read 102. Paul looked weak and exhausted. I told my mother about the ex-lax trick.

"Is that why he's sick?" I asked.

"Hard to say, but I don't think it would have given him a fever," she replied, then paused for effect. "I know you and Larry thought it would be funny playing that trick on your brother, but he got sick and it's not funny."

Everything becomes safer in the clouds.

That evening, my family was together at the dinner table. Paul looked tired and weak. He wouldn't eat anything on his plate. After dinner, I remember my dad standing up. He said, "Children, your mother and I have an exciting announcement to make. I have signed an important contract and we will be moving to the East Coast in six weeks."

My sister, Gretchen, started crying thinking about all her friends she would miss, and her horse she would have to leave behind. I looked at Paul, hoping that he hadn't really understood what it would mean for us having to leave everything we knew and loved in the world.

Paul tried to get up from the dinner table on his own, but it was clear he did not have the strength to walk back to our room.

I am on the cloud again, and in slow motion I watch as my father walks over and picks up my brother Paul. He scoops him up into his arms. They begin to leave the dining room, but for a moment my dad stops and turns around.

He tells my brother to say "goodnight." Then he gently nudges him. At first Paul is too weak to say anything. His eyes are closed at first, but then he gathers what strength he has, opens his eyes, and looks at me. I see the slightest smile, like he is glad to finally be going to sleep, and in the softest of tones, he says something I cannot quite understand, and then he and my dad disappear into the back of the house.

My parents put Paul in my older brother's empty room, and I slept in our bunk bed, but I didn't sleep well without my brother that night, not knowing if he was going to be alright.

The next morning, I learned that my parents had taken Paul to the hospital in the middle of the night. My mom figured out that her thermometer wasn't working, and that his fever was higher than 102. At the hospital, the nurses immediately put Paul in a tub of ice; my mom was right. His temperature was 107.

I went over to Larry's house that morning, and we went to a deserted baseball field near his house, and when we got there I ran away and found a little spot underneath the old bleachers, behind a wall where the trash blew underneath my feet with the wind.

It was the first time in my life that I felt alone, completely alone, there by the empty field in the wind, my little brother packed in ice somewhere. There wasn't anything I could do except feel the wind blow through me, and hope that he would be alright.

As I am writing this, my eyes filled with tears, I realize for the first time that Paul's soul must have been released at that instant in time because I can still remember a little voice saying that I would write about this moment, and I remember that moment now as clearly as it were today and I swear to God it has taken me nearly fifty years to have the courage to write it down like this.

When Larry's mom dropped me off in front of the lonely house, I did not want to knock on the door. I don't remember how long I stood on the porch not wanting to be there.

When the door slowly opened, I saw my father cry for the first time in my life as those words rang out into eternity: "We've lost your little brother."

When I graduated from prep school, seven years later, the editors of the yearbook, not knowing my story, wrote, "John leaves for his home in the clouds." Little did I know, at the time, they were talking about my struggle for self-acceptance.

Everyone could see I was in the clouds but no one knew why, least of all me. Looking back, I spent decades of my life standing on the porch of our house peering through the window, wondering why Paul left me behind and whether I had pushed him away.

The doctors performed an autopsy on Paul's heart shortly after he passed away. They told my parents that the inside of his heart was the size of a walnut, with no chambers. The surgeons called my brother a "medical miracle." It was virtually impossible for him to have been walking and talking with a heart like that.

That moment on the porch wouldn't be the first or the last time that I disassociated from the pain of my reality, and for the next forty years or so I used all sorts of distractions to numb my reality: booze, money, drugs, sex, people, places and things, thoughts and more thoughts— anything to transport me out of the present and the shame that developed around not feeling like I was enough to save my brother, and blaming myself for his passing.

At first, fly fishing was an escape too. I could put everything behind me there on the stream, and that escape became my refuge. It saved my life.

When I was self-consumed by shame and survivor's guilt, I didn't see how "I" had inadvertently taken the place of spirit; by thinking that I could have saved my brother I had replaced God with my own ego. Without knowing it, I left no room for a benevolent source to guide me. When the river showed me how powerless I was over my own brother's death, and frankly how I was powerless over just about anything and everything in this world, God used the most painful moment of my life to become the most transformational.

Back on Cottonwood creek, the sun began to sink behind the mountain and the temperature plummeted. Having finally put this story to paper I sighed with relief and put on my down jacket. I took up my fly rod and I walked over to the creek where Paul and I used to fish. I noticed my breath moving out from my lungs into the air, visible, fading, disappearing then being replaced again and again. A shiver ran up my spine. I sat down to look at the lovely pool below, and then I spoke out loud to him for the first time in nearly five decades.

"Where are you?" I asked.

And out of nowhere, I felt his presence and suddenly I knew that he had never left me; I had left him.

Today, Paul and I talk all the time, and I know he is with me wherever I am. He is my Angel with a Perfect Heart. He was always an angel but I was too busy trying to save him to see how perfect he really was. I always told people that Paul's heart was on the wrong side, but my angel now reminds me that mine is only on the right side when I trust it wholeheartedly.

My angel has shown me that just when I think I know how something is going to turn out, my heart reminds me to let go and let God in. The heart helps us to transform false thinking into numinous food necessary for the growth of spirit.

My angel reminds me that everything is perfect just the way it is. This is the gift of a perfect heart: it counteracts the poison of overly rational thought with the gift of self-acceptance.

When we were younger I taught Paul to fish. Today he is returning the favor by teaching me how to be more grounded, and to live from the heart.

When I am very quiet on the river and present to the glint of sunlight dancing off waters, I know my brother's perfect heart beats within me, contained within the uncontainable that is love.

That night, as my dad carried him away in his arms, my angel told me what he was trying to say:

It wasn't your fault. I love you. Thank you for being my brother.

I am graced by waters.

> *Holy Spirit,*
>
> *You are the truth within us, telling us that we are loved and capable of the kind of love that we only dreamed of. Loving kindness is born from spirit: forgiveness and compassion for what is. Thank You Angel with a Perfect Heart for becoming my protector and releasing me from the past. I love You today as much as I did when I was a child. Thank You for showing us how we can all recover our ability to be connected to spirit.*
>
> *Thank You for the gift of play and my love of the river. May we now use those gifts to become protectors of others, and protectors of the river itself.*

Acknowledgments

To all those in my family who have come before, especially my brothers, Paul and Kresser, who are my angels on this journey home. Special thanks to all who supported me while writing this book: to my parents, Al and Germaine Dietsch, and sister, Gretchen, with love and gratitude. To my children, Sally and Johnny, who help keep me grounded. In particular I would like to thank my beautiful wife, Mollie, who has supported my vision all these years; I could not have written this book without your love, support, and faith.

I would also like to thank all those who helped me to understand our deep connection to the late Norman Maclean and his message of redemption and spirit in his story *A River Runs Through It*: Patrick Markey, Robert Redford, Richard Friedenberg, Joel Snyder, John Maclean, and the late George Croonenberghs, as well as all those who helped me to oversee the fly fishing scenes of the film during the summer of 1991: John Bailey, Jason Borger, Jerry Siem, Bob Auger, and Joe Urbani, as well as many others.

In particular I would like to thank Will Gustafson, a fly fishing client and close friend who read an early draft of my manuscript and, unsolicited, offered to help support this book project financially. Will introduced me to Tom Zenner, and Tom introduced me to Austin Miller, at Miller Dupree, who became my agent and found us a book deal at Post Hill Press. Thanks, guys. There are no coincidences.

Thanks also to my posse: Erik Odom, Stephan B. Poulter, Seth Braun, Randy Dean, Robert Landes, Pat Ashby, Roger Harrell, Clark Stevens, Devin Galaudet, Marvin Trieger, Kip "Bok" Wood, Victor Koeppler, Susan Foxley, Jeff Compton, Lori Hoffman, Laurie Parres, and Zach Rosenblatt.

To the late Georges Odier, John Hollinger, and Chuck Fothergill, my fly fishing mentors. Also, to my fishing mentor Andy Mill who helped get me my first jobs: as a fishing guide and as a TV writer/producer. To Jarrod Hollinger, Paul Jacobson, Gary Hubbell, and all the guides and clients I have fished with at Aspen Outfitting over the last several decades. To all those at NBC Sports and Outdoor Channel, in particular Lloyd Adams, for giving me an opportunity to fish all over the world for my TV series. To all the fly fishing companies that have provided my equipment over the years including Scott Rods, ORVIS, Simms, Galvin, and Rio. To all the conservation organizations, particularly Trout Unlimited, that protect fisheries from the threats that can destroy them (we all need to support these organizations).

May the grace of waters become a channel of transformation for all of us. Tight Lines!

About the Author

JOHN DIETSCH IS AN AWARD-WINNING writer, producer, director, talent, and consultant on hundreds of film and television shows focusing on the outdoors, travel, and fly fishing. As a life coach, teacher, TV personality, Aspen Colorado guide, and host of fly fishing trips across the globe, John helps his clients and students follow their passion by connecting with nature. Dietsch is perhaps best known in fly fishing circles for his supervision, doubling, and stunt work on the fly fishing scenes for the Oscar-winning film *A River Runs Through It*. John's first book and co-author byline, *Shadowcasting*, won a Colorado Book Award. His TV and film productions have garnered more than twenty-three awards, including a Telly. *Graced by Waters* is Dietsch's first collection of stories to celebrate and explore his spiritual connection to waters and the natural world. John is blessed by his beautiful wife Mollie and two adult children, John Jr. and Sarah Elizabeth. Their home is in Pacific Palisades, California.